The British Railways Standard 9F 2–10–0

ISBN 1 871608 29 5

Dedication

For my daughter Rachel

Published by

Irwell Press

15 Lover's Lane Grasscroft Oldham 0L4 4DP

Printed by Amadeus Press, Huddersfield

CONTENTS

The handsome proportions of the high capacity BR 1F tender are clearly apparent in this official view of the first Swindon–built 2–10–0.

The final Crewe–built 9F, No.92250 and the last steam locomotive to be built there (officially reckoned to be the 7,331st), pictured brand new on 14th December 1958. Photographs of the engine with double chimney are comparatively rare as only 6 months later it was rebuilt with the Giesl Ejector, which it retained for the rest of its short life. L.W. Perkins.

Introduction

The British Railways Class 9F 2-10-0s were the last main line steam locomotives to be built in quantity for service in the British Isles, the tail end of about 60,000 so employed over a period of nearly 150 years. They were directly derived from the BR Class 7 mixed traffic 4-6-2 whose evolution and development has earlier been covered in some detail by the present writer in *Britannia – Birth of a Locomotive* (Irwell Press 1991). Whereas the other eleven BR Standard steam locomotive classes (and the 2-10-0 was *not* officially regarded, at first, as *Standard*) were planned simply as modern replacements for a host of long established, existing designs, the 9F by its very power classification broke new ground. Although intended as a heavy goods locomotive, admittedly with a higher operating speed than its countless predecessors, it proved to be remarkably versatile, showing a totally unexpected propensity as an express passenger locomotive!

By the time the first 2-10-0s appeared in 1954 the steam locomotive both in Great Britain and overseas was fighting for its very survival and the wonder is now that so many were built, although it is fair to say that even when the last was completed their swift demise was by no means anticipated. It should also be said that some experiments were made which *at the time,* it was considered, might enable the steam locomotive to hold out a little longer, against the increasingly ferocious economic and social onslaught of the 1950s. These involved an Italian-style boiler, an Austrian exhaust system, and an American stoker, but these trials merely showed that at the end of the day it was difficult to improve upon a well designed basic Stephensonian steam locomotive as originally devised in Britain.

The writer's own enduring memory of the BR 2-10-0s is of invariably grimy, single-chimney Annesley 9Fs in the early 1960s, endlessly trundling back and forth just north of Nottingham, daylight clearly visible under their boilers – thereby living up to their popular nickname of 'spaceships.' He would like to thank his father, Geoffrey Atkins, John Edgington, Hywel Singleton and John Wilson for invaluable assistance, and his wife, Christine for typing the manuscript. John Hooper compiled the allocation and other data in Appendix 5.

C.P.A. Harrogate, March 1993.

The final 9F to appear, 92220, completed at Swindon Works in March 1960. As the last steam locomotive to be built by and for British Railways it was accorded lined green passenger livery, a copper capped double chimney, and the name EVENING STAR, first used 120 years earlier by the former GWR. Author's Collection.

LNER Class P1 3–cylinder 2–8–2 No.2393 hauls an up 100 wagon coal train at Sandy on 8th June 1933. G.H. Soole Collection, NRM.

LMS 2–6–0 + 0–6–2 Beyer Garratt No.4991 heads an up Toton – Brent coal train near Bedford in 1937. Following the arrival of the BR 9F 2–10–0s in quantity on these duties from 1955, the LMS Garratts were rapidly withdrawn from service. P. Ransome Wallis Collection, NRM.

Chapter 1 – A Brief History of the British Goods Locomotive

At the close of the 19th century Great Britain was the wealthiest nation on earth. Its prosperity was largely based on a huge manufacturing industry (the so-called 'Workshop of the World'), which was nevertheless already in perceptible decline. This industry was serviced by an extensive and complex railway network, whose prime function was the conveyance of raw materials, especially coal.

Instrumental in this was the humble inside-cylinder 0-6-0 goods engine, first built as early as 1833 and still being produced in declining numbers until the 1940s. In all some 15,000 engines of this type were constructed for service in Britain, of which about half were in traffic around 1900, when they also accounted for about 40% of the entire British main line locomotive stock.

In 1892 F.W. Webb on the London & North Western Railway produced the first British purpose-built eight-coupled tender locomotive, and within eleven years all the major coal hauling railways in England, except one, had introduced eight-coupled engines. The sole exception was the Midland, who nevertheless at this time actually ordered ten but never built them. Also in 1903 the Great Western Railway built its first 2-8-0, an epoch making locomotive, which was to remain in intermittent production for the next forty years, and would have been *fifty* years later had certain factions had their way! In 1906 one successfully worked a special test train of 2012 tons, whilst regularly during World War II they worked 100

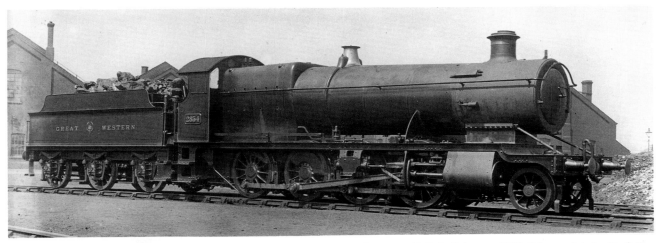

A Churchward GWR 2–8–0 in its prime. No.2854 at Old Oak Common when new. Built in February 1913, it is resplendent in fully lined out passenger green livery and copper capped chimney, both permanently suppressed on GWR goods engines after 1914. It is superheated and carries the newly developed boiler top feed. NRM.

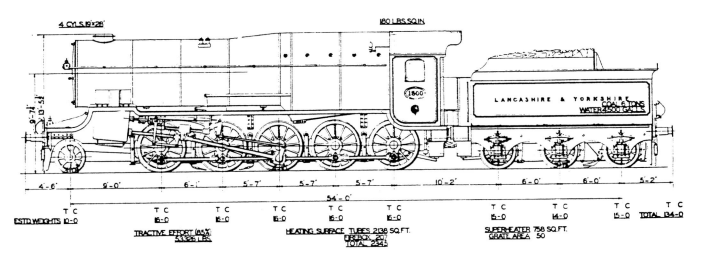

The first British 2–10–0 was proposed by the Lancashire & Yorkshire Railway for the Goole coal traffic as early as June 1914. Clearly inspired by the huge Belgian four–cylinder 2–10–0s designed by J.B. Flamme, it was one of a range of designs then being considered by George Hughes which also included a four–cylinder simple 2–8–2, and four–cylinder compound 2–8–0. All these projects were killed by the outbreak of World War 1, although the 2–10–0 was briefly re-examined by the newly formed LMS ten years later.

wagon trains in the Thames Valley.

By 1914 British coal output reached what proved to be its all time peak of nearly 300 million tons *per annum* and on the eve of World War I the Lancashire & Yorkshire Railway was actively contemplating a large four-cylinder 2-10-0, whilst the Great Central was appraising a possible 2-10-2. Neither was ever built, but around 1922 Nigel Gresley on the Great Northern Railway also envisaged a 2-10-2, which subsequently emerged in somewhat truncated form three years later as the two LNER P1 three-cylinder 2-8-2s. Also equipped with auxiliary boosters on the trailing truck they were the most powerful non-articulated British goods engines ever built, and could theoretically handle 1600 tons between Peterborough and London. However, in practice, they proved to be something of an operational liability and both were scrapped after only twenty years, in 1945.

Also faced with the problem of working heavy London-bound coal trains with only one locomotive (to keep down crew costs) and to comply with weight limitations, the LMS resorted to the Beyer Garratt, in somewhat cumbersome 2-6-0 + 0-6-2 form, which could easily have been a lot better than it was. Meanwhile, the LMS was also struggling to produce an effective eight-coupled heavy freight locomotive for more general use. This was finally achieved in 1935 by its new Chief Mechanical Engineer, William Stanier, in the shape of his Class 8F 2-8-0, which owed more than a little to the Churchward 28XX 2-8-0 on the GWR, whence Stanier had come.

BRITISH RAILWAYS FREIGHT TRAIN REVENUE & MILEAGE 1948 – 1968

Year	Total Freight Revenue £	Coal & Mineral Revenue £	Total Loaded Freight Mileage	Steam Hauled Loaded Freight Mileage
1948	180,804,000	96,720,000	118,396,000	—
1949	179,002,000	97,774,000	119,341,000	—
1950	198,917,000	110,318,000	123,709,000	—
1951	227,858,000	128,081,000	125,807,000	—
1952	250,537,000	143,874,000	123,801,000	—
1953	263,083,000	154,250,000	123,583,000	—
1954	272,838,000	161,990,000	122,337,000	121,486,000
1955	274,224,000	168,158,000	115,809,000	114,257,000
1956	284,066,000	178,642,000	117,215,000	115,619,000
1957	288,517,000	181,508,000	117,906,000	116,185,000
1958	259,103,000	167,059,000	110,065,000	108,305,000
1959	241,082,000	153,336,000	107,260,000	103,000,000
1960	247,320,000	157,512,000	108,423,000	98,703,000
1961	236,842,000	147,819,000	104,854,000	90,265,000
1962	224,444,000	140,190,000	96,198,000	74,854,000
1963	235,384,000	142,294,000	91,601,000	60,988,000
1964	232,981,000	141,903,000	87,574,000	46,503,000
1965	225,513,000	138,880,000	77,518,000	28,209,000
1966	216,921,000	133,930,000	68,013,000	14,916,000
1967	194,824,000	118,785,000	61,011,000	6,488,000
1968	204,334,000	124,448,000	60,250,000	711,000

Stanier 8F 2–8–0 built at Brighton in September 1944 for the LNER as class O6. It became an LMS engine in October 1947 renumbered as 8729.

A Vulcan Foundry 'Austerity' of 1944 seen in BR ownership in April 1951. This example lasted until August 1966.

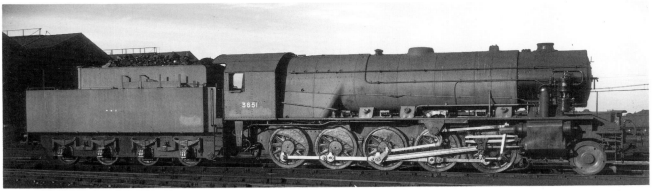

Riddles 'Austerity' 2–10–0 for the War Department, No.3651, pictured at Doncaster in 1943 whilst being run in. This engine later went to the Longmoor Military Railway and is now preserved on the Severn Valley Railway as No.600 GORDON. A total of 150 engines of this type was built by the North British Loco. Co. between 1943 and 1945. As regards the coupled wheel flange and coupling rod arrangements, the design provided guidelines for the later BR 9F – quite apart from demonstrating that within the British loading gauge it was possible to accommodate a wide firebox above coupled wheels. NRM.

The BR Class 9F 2–10–0 when it appeared represented the first major advance in British steam freight locomotive design for 50 years, 'special' types excluded. Just how much larger in size than the outstanding Churchward 2–8–0 is graphically shown here with the prototype No.92000, newly outshopped with double chimney, and former GWR No.2865, standing outside 'A' Shop at Swindon Works on 21st February 1960. (No.92220 was just being completed inside at this time). T.E. Williams Collection NRM.

The 8F was initially selected for emergency wartime production for service overseas, but it was not a cheap engine to build. Robert Riddles, Stanier's right-hand man, was requested by the Ministry of Supply to develop a less expensive version for the War Department. With parallel round-topped in place of taper Belpaire boiler, and fabricated components rather than castings where these were possible, the result was the 'Austerity' 2-8-0. A total of 935 were built by the North British Locomotive Co. and Vulcan Foundry between 1943 and 1945, of which 733 were eventually purchased and operated by British Railways, others remaining overseas.

Riddles also developed his 2-8-0 into a 2-10-0 with wide firebox whose maximum axleload was only 13½ tons com-pared to the 15 tons of the eight-coupled engine. 150 of these 2-10-0s, likewise conforming to the British loading gauge, were built by NBL, of which 25 were later acquired by BR. These led rather obscure lives in southern Scotland where, rather oddly, Stanier 2-8-0s were always a rarity. Some of the WD 2-10-0s worked on the LMS and LNER on loan during and after the war.

By the end of 1949 British Railways was well supplied with 2-8-0s just about two thousand in fact, or ten per cent of the total locomotive stock, many of them built during the previous ten years. As a consequence withdrawal commenced in 1949 of the Fowler LMS Class 7F 0-8-0s introduced only twenty years earlier and far from life expired. What was now required was not yet more eight-coupled heavy freight engines in the traditional mould, but a design having enhanced boiler capacity capable of sustaining higher speeds up the banks and on the level.

BRITISH FREIGHT LOCOMOTIVE TRENDS 1913 – 1965

Year	Wheel	Arrangement.			Total	Total
31st Dec	0–6–0	0–8–0	2–8–0	2–10–0		UK Steam
1913	7,387	864	208	0	8,459	23,664
1922	6,742	1,234	337	0	8,313	23,891
1927*	6,447	1,181	665	2	8,295	23,877
1937*	4,753	1,032	733	2	6,520	19,689
1947	4,383	952	1,469	0	6,804	20,033
1950	3,935	566	2,021	25	6,547	19,598
1953	3,521	455	1,999	25	6,000	18,584
1956	3,159	434	1,979	140	5,712	17,522
1959	2,307	281	1,895	273	4,756	14,452
1962	843	127	1,618	251	2,839	8,767
1965	105	40	783	170	1,098	2,989

The two 2–10–0s listed for 1927 and 1937 were represented by the LNER Class P1 2–8–2.

NB. Almost throughout, the proportion of freight tender locomotives of total stock was remarkably consistent at around 33 per cent.

Comparative Table of Leading Dimensions of the BR Class 9F 2–10–0 and its Antecedents

Introduced	1903	1935	1943	1943	1954
Railway	GWR	LMS	WD/MOS	WD/MOS	BR
Class	28XX*	8F	Austerity	Austerity	9F
Wheel arrangement	2–8–0	2–8–0	2–8–0	2–10–0	2–10–0
Cylinders (2).	18½" x 30"	18½" x 28"	19" x 28"	19" x 28"	20" x 28"
Driving wheel dia.	4' 7½"	4' 8½"	4' 8½"	4' 8½"	5' 0"
Boiler Pressure	225lb	225lb	225lb	225lb	250lb
Evap H.S. ft^2	1841	1650	1680	1951	2015
Superheater ft^2	253	215	310	423	535
Grate Area ft^2	27.1	28.7	28.6	40.0	40.2
Adhesive Wt. tons	67.5	63.1	61.25	67.15	77.5
Engine Wt. tons	75.5	72.1	70.25	78.3	86.7
Tractive Effort	35,380lb	32,438lb	34,215lb	34,215lb	39,667lb

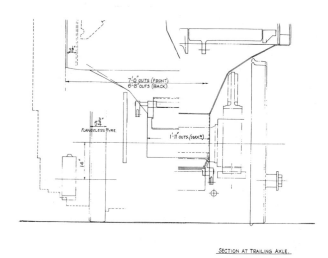

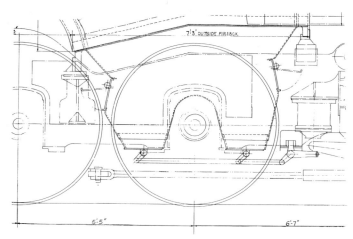

SECTION AT TRAILING AXLE.

Crucial development drawings by F.G. Carrier, showing how an adequate ashpan could be accommodated beneath a shallow wide firebox mounted above 5 ft. diameter coupled wheels. Dated 17th July 1951, Riddles had already by this time decided in favour of the 2–10–0 option.

The original comparative tractive effort/speed curves for the ex–LMS 8F 2–8–0 and BR 2–8–2/2–10–0 alternatives. Despite its greater initial starting tractive effort it will be seen that above 18 mph its drawbar pull fell below that of the 2–8–2 which on this basis, due to its larger boiler, was a more attractive proposition. In order to make a stronger case for the 2–10–0 the data was 're–calculated'; the 2–10–0 curve obligingly remained above and did not fall below the corresponding 2–8–2 curve (see opposite).

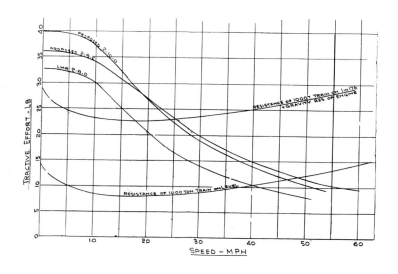

Chapter 2 – 2–8–2 or 2–10–0?

The Gresley P1 2-8-2s had been something of an operational embarrassment because they could haul longer trains than could be accommodated in existing sidings and refuge loops. The various 2-8-0 designs could start away with and haul any trains of *convenient* length, at somewhat pedestrian speeds commensurate with unbraked loose-coupled stock. Under the newly nationalised regime there was at last the long overdue prospect of working freights composed of modern continuously braked stock, which meant increased operating speeds. To achieve this greater boiler power was required than was achievable with the 27 – 30 sq. ft. narrow grates of the existing 2-8-0 engines, none of whose coupled wheels exceeded 4ft. 9in. diameter.

E.S. Cox's outline proposal in June 1948 was for a 2-8-2 with wide (36 sq. ft.) grate and 5ft. 3in. coupled wheels, to be made interchangeable as regards boiler, cylinders, motion and hind truck, with his projected 'light' Class 5 4-6-2. Initially, however, design resources were concentrated on the ten mixed traffic tender and tank locomotive classes, and the more specialised heavy freight and heavy passenger designs were deferred until well into 1950 when tentative thoughts were first accorded them.

R.C. Bond had been instrumental in getting the 'light' 4-6-2 uprated to Class 6, whilst R.A. Riddles as Chief proclaimed his desire to build a 2-10-0 rather than a 2-8-2 heavy freight engine in the light of his wartime 'Austerity' 2-10-0 produced for the Ministry of Supply. Cox responded in a lengthy memorandum giving *ten* reasons why the 2-8-2 was to be preferred, the 'Austerity' dimensions being taken to represent the 2-10-0 option...

Memorandum

11th August 1950

Large Freight Locomotive

The 2-10-0 locomotive has certain definite advantages as applied to the kind of mineral train schedules hitherto in force on British Railways – schedules calling for average speeds of 17 to 25 m.p.h. with maximum of 40 m.p.h.
There are ten good reasons why it is not the most suitable type for the higher level of performance now envisaged, calling for average speeds of 35 m.p.h. with maxima of 50 m.p.h. The 2-8-2 type is more suitable, and for the following reasons:-
(1) The 2-10-0 is absolutely limited by the British Loading Gauge to a wheel diameter at 4'10". At 50 m.p.h. 18% less Tractive Effort is available in comparison with a 2-8-2 having 5'6" wheels as under:-

Wheel Dia	R.P.M. at 50 m.p.h.	M.E.P. as % of Boiler pressure	Available TE at 50 m.p.h. (based on 36000lbs starting TE
4' 10"	263	21.0%	8900 lbs
5' 6"	231	24.8%	10500 lbs

No greater starting Tractive Effort than at present available is required, siding lengths will not admit longer trains. What is required is much more T.E. at speed.
(2) The future lies with faster freight services. The 2-10-0 because of its limited speed/power factor, has less potential to meet future conditions. It has less to offer as an alternative to electrification.
(3) The boiler, heart of the locomotive, is severely and artificially restricted in the 2-10-0. Due to the need to carry the firebox above the coupled wheel, maximum barrel diameter can only be 5'9⅞" as against 6'5½" with a 2-8-2.

(4) On the 2-10-0 free area through the tube bank is 4·56ft² or 11.4% of grate area. The 2-8-2 gives 6.79ft² free area or 16.2% of grate area. All experience shows that a percentage of 15 or over is necessary to ensure that the tube bank can absorb the maximum heat the grate is able to release.
(5) Firebox volume, important with some types of coal, is only 202ft³ for a 2-10-0 as against 273ft³ for a 2-8-2. No advantage can be gained by increasing length of combustion chamber still further in case of 2-10-0 since this does not apply volume where it is principally required, i.e. above grate at point of greatest admixture of air and combustion gases. Moreover such a modification would reduce the sheer capacity of the boiler to boil water due to loss of heating surface.
(6) For high rates of working and long runs, ample ashpan capacity is essential. This cannot be provided on the 2-10-0. Ashpan volume on 2-10-0 is only 38ft³ as compared with 49ft³ on 2-8-2. Moreover the part of the ashpan over the wheels is shallow and it is not self-cleaning so that a progressive diminution of effective grate area on long non-stop runs can be anticipated. This has not happened on present day schedules with 2-10-0s because only low boiler power outputs are called for and frequent stops allow the condition of the pan over the wheels to be examined and cleared if necessary.
(7) The 2-10-0 with five axles loaded at 13½ tons does not give better adhesion and braking features than the 2-8-2 with four coupled axles loaded at 17½ tons. The adhesion weight of the 2-10-0 is restricted as much by the limited size of boiler it is possible to fit as by axle weight limitation.
(8) Although with roller bearing boxes the difference may be only marginal, the 2-10-0 does have a higher internal resistance than the 2-8-2, and in starting heavy trains, every pound of the total cylinder effort which can go to moving the train instead of the engine itself is of value.
(9) The 2-8-2 can be built up out of the same standard components as the 4-6-2 locomotives now under design, and can use the same flanging blocks, patterns and components except in the case of side rods and wheels. To modernise and make the most of the W.D. 2-10-0 will require a considerable number of items particular to this engine class only.
(10) Finally, it is worth while to survey the world at large. With increasing demands for power at speed the ten coupled engine is vanishing and the eight coupled engine holds the field.

U.S.A.
The railways were badly caught out in the middle thirties when road competition forced an increase in freight speeds. The many thousands of engines with wheels from 4'6" diameter to 5'0" diameter including 2-10-0 engines in large numbers, were inadequate for the job and construction thereafter took the form of 2-8-4 and 4-8-4 with wheels from 5'6" to 6'0". Where still more power was required the Americans have invariably preferred the articulated type with six or eight coupled units rather than develop further the ten coupled type.

France
The 2-10-0 has had a certain vogue, here again connected with relatively low speeds. The most successful general purpose engine the French Railways have ever had is the American 2-8-2 type of which over 1300 units have been supplied since the war. Fitted with mechanical stokers, or oil burning and with virtually no limit to steam production capacity, these engines are giving performances previously unheard of in French practice. (see *Revue Generale de Chemins de Fer* January 1950).

Germany
The 2-10-0 had been a standard type but only with 4'7" diameter wheels and associated with moderate speeds.

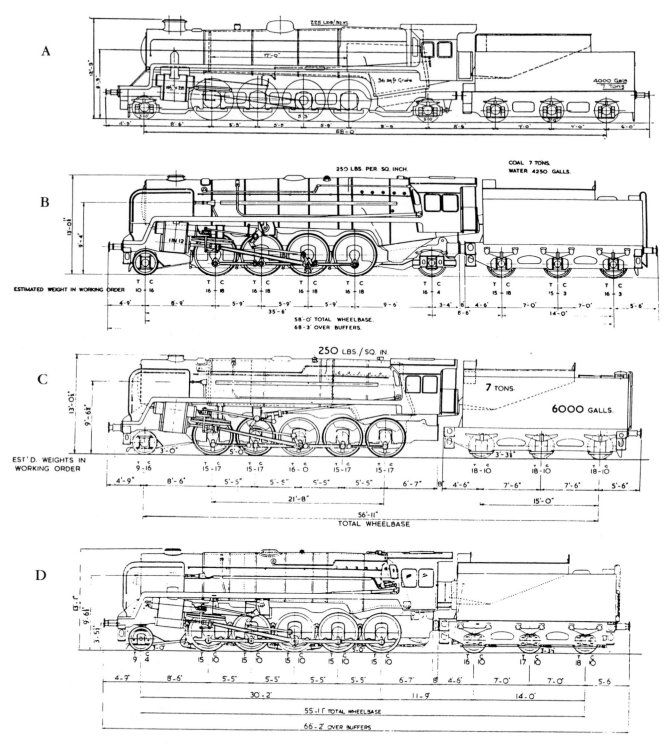

The Evolution of the 9F

A. **Original early 1948 scheme for Class 8 2–8–2 with bar frames, boiler, cylinders, motion, and hind truck interchangeable with proposed Class 5 mixed traffic Pacific.** B. **Proposed 2–8–2 directly derived from Class 7 mixed traffic 4–6–2. Early 1951.** C. **The 2–10–0 (then still referred to as Class 8) as envisaged in late 1951, with smokebox regulator, I–section coupling rods, and (by implication) roller bearings on all axles. The projected 6000 gallon tender is also shown. The 'Austerity' pattern chimney appeared on official diagrams as late as November 1953.** D. **The 9F 2–10–0 as completed in late 1953, with dome regulator, plain bearings, and plain–section coupling rods. Note saving in weight and handsome 'Britannia' style chimney.**

The welded ashpan and rocking grate assembly for a 9F 2–10–0. Of necessity built to a different shape to that of the BR Standard 4–6–2s, cubic capacity at 55 ft was actually greater than the 50 ft. of the Class 7 4–6–2 ashpan. NRM.

India

The 2-10-0 has not been built for many years but the 2-8-2 with 5′1½″ wheels was a pre-war Indian standard and an entirely new and up-to-date version is now being built at the North British Locomotive Co.

Australia

Ten coupled engines are unknown; 2-8-2 or 4-8-2 cover latest construction.

Narrow Gauge Lines

The 4-8-2 or 2-8-2 has become almost a world wide standard because of the ample firebox dimensions permitted. When larger locomotives are required the Garratt type is adopted with 6 or 8 coupled wheels in each unit.

There the matter rested for the time being, but by early 1951 the first BR Class 7 4-6-2s were newly in traffic and Derby was able to look at the question of the heavy freight engine. Some quite detailed work was initially done on the 2-8-2 which was to be made interchangeable as far as possible with the 4-6-2, particularly as regards the boiler, cylinders and valve gear. Indeed a complete motion arrangement was drawn out, with the cylinders simply more steeply inclined, at 1 in 12 compared to the 1 in 24 of the larger wheeled 4-6-2. Some scheming was done to see whether clasp brakes could be accommodated on the hind truck in order to increase the braking capacity, a common practice overseas, but the proposed arrangement did not meet with satisfaction.

Riddles, however, persisted in his request that a 2-10-0 be evolved; F.G. Carrier's initial diagram, dated 20th June 1951,

represented a distinct improvement upon the 'Austerity' with which he had himself earlier been involved. Remarkably the boiler proportions were much better despite the fact that coupled wheel diameter had been increased from 4ft 8-½n. to 5ft. 0in., and within the confines of the British loading gauge every inch counted. (Frank Carrier was a locomotive designer in the true sense; a resident of Derby Drawing Office since late Midland Railway days he had produced the initial diagram for the LMS 'Royal Scot' 4-6-0 back in November 1926, and the bold styling of the BR Standards was due to him). Eight days later E.S. Cox produced a further memorandum on the large freight locomotive which this time found in favour of the 2-10-0 rather than the 2-8-2. This *volte face* seems to have been in recognition of the fact that the new engines were urgently required to work existing, unfitted, freight stock, at the long established maximum speed of 40mph rather than the 50 mph anticipated a year earlier...

Memorandum

28th June 1951

Large Freight Locomotive

A freight engine of greater capacity than any existing type having been called for by several Regions on the 1953 Programme, the following submits a proposal for a suitable design and sets out the various considerations which have been taken into account.

It has been assumed on the operating side –

(a) That no greater length and weight of trains than at present have to be considered, due to length of available sidings. The 1,000 ton mineral train has, therefore, been taken as the basis for calculation.

(b) That while the locomotive should be capable of running at 50 m.p.h. with fitted trains of lighter weight, on 1,000 ton mineral trains no greater speed than 40 m.p.h. need be considered with unfitted stock, wagons with grease axleboxes requiring to be limited to this speed.

(c) Arising from (a) and (b) above, the problem is one of reducing overall timings by raising speeds on up grades and on level rather than running any faster downhill.

(d) If (c) is accepted then no special problems of braking arise with non-fitted wagons.

On the locomotive side the following premises have been made –

(1) That a straightforward non-articulated locomotive should be considered.

(2) That two cylinders only should be used for simplicity of shed examination and maintenance.

(3) That B.R. Standard design should be followed as far as possible.

From the foregoing, two alternative types of locomotive are possible:-

1. A 2-8-2, having the same boiler as the Standard Class 7, 4-6-2 type. This would have 5'3" coupled wheels, 35,916lb. Tractive Effort and a factor of adhesion of 4.22 with maximum axle weight of 17 tons.

2. A 2-10-0 having a wide firebox boiler about halfway in size between those on the Classes 6 and 7 Standard 4-6-2s, coupled wheels 5'0" dia. 39,666lb Tractive Effort factor of adhesion of 4.5 with maximum axleweight of 16 tons.

Choice as between 2-8-2 and 2-10-0

In comparative dimensions and ratios, the advantage lies with the 2-10-0 for the type of duties envisaged. The principal reasons are –

(i) More tractive effort at all speeds.

(ii) Better adhesion and more economical use of available weight.

(iii) Lower first cost of engine since weight is less.

(iv) The wheel diameter is 3" less. With modern valve events and roller bearings this is no detriment. 50 m.p.h. with a 5'0" dia. wheel corresponds to 60 m.p.h. with 6'2" wheels as on Class 7, 4-6-2, a speed which these latter engines readily attain.

(v) The slightly smaller boiler as compared with the Class 7, 4-6-2 will none the less supply all the steam needed under freight conditions. A number of new flanging blocks will, however, be required.

(vi) With flangeless tyres on the driving wheels it has been proved with the W.D. locomotive that easy negotiation of curves down to 4½ chains is assured. A slightly increased sideplay is required on leading and trailing coupled wheels.

(vii) The ashpan arrangement is not so good, but its capacity is at least as great as the 2-8-2 and the arrangement of its sloping sides somewhat better than on the L.M.R. 'Duchess' class for example.

The advantage for the 2-10-0, which could be expected to disappear at the higher speeds due to the smaller wheel, is maintained because the greater adhesive weight permits the 2-10-0 to have a 20 × 28 cylinder as against the 19½ × 28 which is the maximum for the 2-8-2.

Choice as between proposed 2-10-0 and existing types.

It will be noted that the starting Tractive Effort of the 2-10-0 is only slightly higher than that of the larger Regional 2-8-0s. but the performance at speed is higher pro rata due to the greater steam producing capacity of the boiler. The principal advantage of the 2-10-0 is its ability to climb the banks faster. At a speed in the neighbourhood of 20 m.p.h., ability to climb 10 m.p.h. faster represents a much greater saving in journey time than would ability to run say 50 m.p.h. instead of 40 m.p.h. downhill. The proposed engine should, therefore,

allow of overall journey times being reduced without increase in maximum speed so far as non-fitted trains are concerned.

Capacity of 2-10-0 in relation to future operating policy.

With fitted mineral trains of 1,000 tons the engine will give the same performance as indicated on the chart uphill, but can travel on the level up to the balancing speed given by the available Tractive Effort which is in the neighbourhood of 50 m.p.h. Downhill speeds may be run probably up to the limit possible with fitted 4-wheel mineral wagons, a value yet to be determined by forthcoming brake trials.

If any higher performance is required under steam traction, the Garratt type locomotive and mechanical stoker will be required, since the Civil Engineers' weight and loading gauge restrictions preclude use of a larger normal locomotive type.

On 17th July 1951 the monthly meeting of Regional Locomotive Chief Draughtsmen was advised that 'Mr. Riddles had concurred with the Chief Officer (Motive Power) that the 2-10-0 was to be adopted in preference to the 2-8-2 as it had the balance of advantages for the duties envisaged'.

Much of the credit for the subsequent success of the 2-10-0 was assuredly due to Frank Carrier, who sadly did not live to see it, dying at the relatively early age of 53 in December 1952, greatly mourned by all who had known him. There was a further irony in that its chief protagonist, Robert Riddles, retired in September 1953, in protest at and coincident with the abolition of the Railway Executive, just as assembly of the prototype was *commencing* at Crewe. There remained, however, a belief that the wrong decision had been taken. Writing his memoirs twenty five years later, Riddles' second in command, Roland Bond, recorded* 'had the decision been mine to make the new standard heavy freight locomotive would have been the 2-8-2. It would I believed, have done all that the 2-10-0 would do'.

A Lifetime with Locomotives by R.C. Bond, Goose & Son Publishers Ltd 1975.

(below & opposite) **Two views of that wide firebox overhang.**

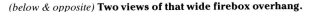

No.92003 brand new at Crewe Works in January 1954. Officially rated Class 9 in February 1952 the BR 2–10–0s with a starting tractive effort of almost 40,000lb were the most powerful two–cylinder locomotives ever to operate in Britain. In recognition of this power, in mid–1953 the late George Dow suggested that the forthcoming engines be accorded suitable names in order to glamorize the freight side of BR's business. In this he was over–ruled by the other two members of the BR Locomotive Naming Committee, E.S. Cox and D.S.M. Barrie. In recent years the naming of diesel locomotives dedicated to freight service has become commonplace.

The balance weights on the 9Fs were largely cosmetic. In reality the reciprocating balance was concentrated in the centre drivers, actually at an angle of 135 degrees to the main crank, and thereby in the same phase on both sides of the engine. This sophisticated technique was developed by Brighton from the system originally employed on the Bulleid Southern three–cylinder 4–6–2s. No.92203 is actually shown after private purchase in 1967, carrying BR mixed traffic lined black (LNW style) livery, never worn in service.

Chapter 3 – Design Development

Production design of the new heavy freight engine began at Brighton Drawing Office under R.G. Jarvis immediately the 2-8-2/2-10-0 question had been resolved. Derby remained responsible for designing the wheels, axles, journals, springs, pony truck and so on, as well as the various tenders. Although still derived from the Class 7 4-6-2 the only major components that were directly interchangeable were the connecting rods and Walschaerts valve gear. Indeed so much new design work was required that when the first 2-10-0s eventually appeared two and a half years later it was officially indicated that they were not regarded as a part of the Standard locomotive range.

Several features of the initial batch of 4-6-2s which it was originally intended to incorporate likewise in the 2-10-0s were progressively abandoned in the light of operating experience with the mixed traffic engines.

The 2-10-0s were to have had roller bearings on all axles, but in February 1952 Riddles had questioned the justification of those on the 4-6-2s, which resulted in later batches having various combinations of roller and plain bearings. In view of the high reliability of modern plain bearings it was decided that these would suffice on the 2-10-0s.

Another 'luxury' on the 4-6-2s, which in February 1952 it was also decided not to perpetuate in the 2-10-0s was the heavy, complex and expensive Melesco multiple valve smoke-box regulator, incorporated in the superheater header. This had originally been specified for the 4-6-2s back in 1948 on account of the potential 'slippery' nature of that wheel arrangement when starting away, which was not so much the case with a high adhesion freight locomotive. A horizontal grid-type regulator high in the vestigial dome was therefore specified, which was not without its initial problems, as will be seen.

Aside from a reduced capital cost, these two major design changes resulted also in an appreciable reduction in engine weight of 2½ tons (from 89·2 to 86·7) and in maximum axleload from 16 to 15½ tons. This in turn had the happy result of reducing the LNER-style Route Availability from RA8 to RA7 which therefore brought it into line with the Class 7 4-6-2. The highest static axleload on the 2-10-0 was not on the engine itself but on the tender, up to 18½ tons.

The 4-6-2s had been provided with cabs mounted directly on the back of the boiler, with the cab floor projecting over the front of the tender. This arrangement had been devised with the best of intentions and after preliminary wind tunnel tests with scale models; despite this, in practice extremely draughty conditions were experienced on the footplate. In later 4-6-2s, and in the 2-10-0s although the cab continued to be attached to the boiler, a return was made to the traditional hinged fall plate folding down from the front of the tender, which produced more comfortable results.

The 4-6-2s had shown an early tendency to bend and break their I-section coupling rods, which were thereafter rede-signed in plain section. The design of these rods for the 2-10-0, which was likewise undertaken at Doncaster, was the sub-ject of considerable debate. At 21ft 8in. the rigid wheelbase was 8/9 inches longer than that of the only two previous ten-coupled tender locomotive designs to have worked in Britain, and in the end it was decided to copy those of the WD 2-10-0s, likewise in plain sections. It was no doubt significant that at the very time the 9F rods were being designed (May 1952) ex-WD 2-10-0 No. 90763 was briefly reallocated to Doncaster

shed.

In the WD engines reciprocating balance had been omitted altogether, but in designing this at 40% in the new BR 2-10-0 Brighton devised a sophisticated technique of cross balancing, permitting a significant (200lb) saving in lead weights in the main driving wheels and, thereby, hammerblow. Resultant riding qualities were legendary, even at speeds 50% greater than the maximum 60mph originally envisaged.

The centre wheels were also to have slightly wider (5¾") flangeless tyres but the fine details of the actual profile were not settled until after experimentation with the first engines in traffic, and that of the ex-LNWR G2 0-8-0 was copied. The second and fourth coupled wheels were provided with 'thin' flanges and those of the leading and trailing axles were turned to standard thickness. The ensemble worked very well with engines commonly running 100,000 miles, or roughly speaking from one general repair to the next, between tyre turning.

The main frames were particularly robust, being cut from 1¼in. steel plate, set over the centres of the coupled axle journals as in the 4-6-2s. The frames were rigidly cross-braced horizontally and were reinforced by supplementary stiffening plates at the back end to compensate for potential weak points below the front of the firebox. The frames of early 2-10-0s at Crewe were cut with an oxy-coal gas flame on a Hancock machine, but later frames were cut with a 'state of the art' Monopol flame cutter which worked off a 1/100 scale negative of the frame slotting working drawing.

Early Crewe 2-10-0s, and all those built at Swindon, had hornguides welded to the frames, but at Crewe's own request, to provide work in its steel foundry, later 2-10-0s built there had cast steel horns riveted to the frames.

This same foundry produced the cylinders for all 251 2-10-0s. These were very similar to those of the 4-6-2s but because of leading crank pin/crosshead clearances on the 2-10-0s these had to be set at slightly wider (1½in) centres. This entailed the production of modified patterns as ¾in. thick distance pieces were ruled out on weight grounds.

Carrier's preliminary diagram showed an elegant 'Britan-nia' type chimney, but Riddles subsequently decided to impose a personal trade mark by substituting the distinctive WD 'Austerity' 2-8-0/2-10-0 style chimney. The necessary draw-ing for this was duly produced at Brighton in early February 1952, and was still shown on diagrams as late as November 1953, by which time Riddles had retired. As completed at Crewe in late December 1953 No.92000 sported a handsome chimney of the type originally proposed. The mystery is that the appropriate Brighton drawing was dated 15th December 1953 i.e. barely a week before, but when questioned on this in late 1991, Mr. E.S. Cox had no recollection whatever of this particular matter, which was never discussed by the design committee.

Specific batches of 2-10-0s built for particular Regions accordingly differed in detail quite apart from the obvious variations in tender type. Thus engines for the WR were fitted with ATC (Automatic Train Control) apparatus in their cabs, Nos. 92045 – 92049 for the LMR were provided with continu-ous blow down. ER and WR engines were provided with 'local' patterns of firehole door, although such considerations for local tradition did not extend to arranging the WR engines for right-hand rather than left-hand drive!

No.92002 under construction in Crewe Works Erecting Shop, late 1953.

92001 is recorded in a slightly more advanced stage of construction at Crewe, late 1953. Note that the engine has been wheeled but that the motion has not yet been set up.

Chapter 4 – Building Programmes

The Class 9F 2-10-0s ultimately accounted for 251 out of the 1047 British Railways Standard steam locomotives originally authorised, and the 999 actually built. In terms of capital expenditure their combined cost of about £7½ million (in contemporary currency) amounted to roughly one third of the £24 million thus spent. The latter figure was spread over the period October 1949 to March 1960, compared to no less than £42 million spent on 750 new diesels in the year 1960 alone.

The first 2-10-0 had appeared precisely one year earlier, and only 32 had been completed, before the public announcement in January 1955 of the BR Re-equipment and Modernization Plan, which foreshadowed the end of steam traction on BR. Nevertheless over 150 additional 2-10-0s were *subsequently* authorised, whose delivery was distinctly protracted due to continuing severe steel shortages and during which dieselisation rapidly accelerated. Freight traffic produced more revenue than passenger services for BR prior to 1969 and steam locomotives operated more than 50% of the freight mileage until 1964.

The 1951 and 1952 Locomotive Building Programmes had been approved in November 1949 and January 1951 respectively before a single example of the BR Standard *marque* had proved itself in traffic. However, over one hundred engines to six different designs had entered service by late November 1951, when an initial order for thirty 2-10-0s was included in the 1953 Programme. This would include ten or fifteen engines which it was intended to equip with the Italian Franco-Crosti boiler. The provisional distribution included no fewer than twenty 2-10-0s, then officially referred to as Class 8s, for the Western Region, with the remaining ten to be equally divided between the Eastern and *Southern* Regions.

Neither the Southern Region nor the Southern Railway before it had ever found the need for an *eight coupled* freight engine and so this would have been an interesting development. However, by July 1952 these five engines were earmarked for the London Midland Region instead.

Even before Crewe Works had made much active progress on building any of the initial batch it received an order for a further 67 2-10-0s in December 1952, for construction in the 1954 Programme. The provisional distribution was to be ER 35, LMR 15, NER 7 and WR 10. Thus by the beginning of 1953, when the first was expected to be completed around August, the Western Region had no fewer than thirty 2-10-0s in prospect.

Though only 53 9Fs were built at Swindon, as against 198 by Crewe, views of them actively under construction at the former works are, nonetheless, curiously scarce. By 1959 Swindon was the only locomotive works in Britain, either railway or private, still building main line steam locomotives, but not for much longer. On 26th July No.92211 is seen in an advanced stage of construction in 'A' Shop. The steep 1 in 8 inclination of the cylinders, in order to clear the loading gauge, is particularly apparent. P.J. Kelley.

LUBRICATION CHART FOR THE BASIC BR CLASS 9F 2-10-0 WITH BR 1F TENDER.
(left-hand side)

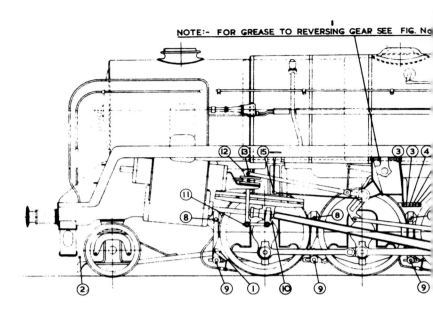

NOTE:- FOR GREASE TO REVERSING GEAR SEE FIG. No

The construction of Crewe's final steam locomotive was recorded photographically. The 2–10–0's boiler is swung through the Erecting Shop, already showing signs of things to come with 350 HP 0–6–0 diesel shunters under construction. R. Partridge Collection.

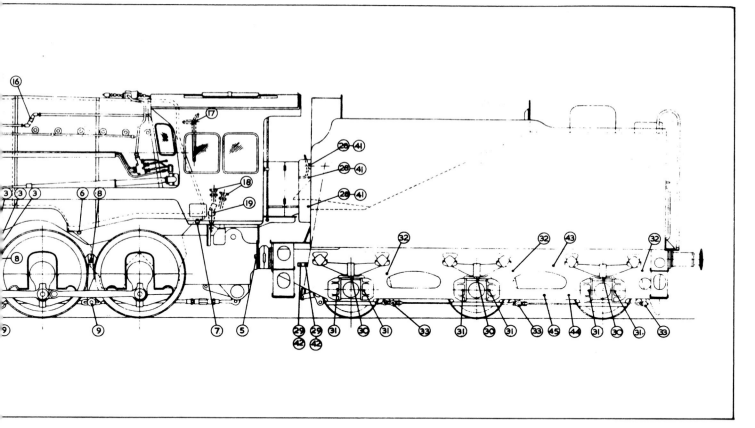

Five years after Nationalization the Western Region had still not fully come to terms with the fact that it was no longer the *Great* Western *Railway*. It had already displayed antipathy toward the new Class 7 4-6-2s, and now it made a reasoned case for permission to build new Churchward 28XX 2-8-0s, to replace older engines life expired at over the 45 year mark. The basic design dated back no less than fifty years, but in superheated form in 1948 it had returned the most economical coal consumption of any of the heavy freight designs tested in the Regional Exchange Trials. It was calculated that at current prices Swindon could build the 2-8-0 at £14,150 apiece, as against an anticipated cost of £23,500 for a 2-10-0. Furthermore, annual operating costs were estimated to be £400 lower.

Robert Riddles took premature retirement in September 1953, when the frames for the first 2-10-0 were just being laid at Crewe, to be succeeded by Roland Bond who was styled Chief Mechanical Engineer. Bond clearly felt he had a rebellion on his hands which needed to be dealt with firmly. He recalled the matter in his memoirs without identifying the Region in question, and referred to having a new 2-8-0 designed, should this be necessary.

In fact *two* alternative 2-8-0 proposals were schemed out in late November 1953. A 2-8-0 version of the Standard Class 5 4-6-0 but with boiler pressure increased from 225 to 250lb was drawn up at RE headquarters whilst Derby Development office sketched out a truncated 9F with shortened boiler and slightly longer firebox.

Only a few days later the Works and Equipment Committee minuted on 8th December 1953: "Locomotive Building and Condemnation Programmes 1953, 1954 and 1955 – Heavy Freight Locomotives. Alteration in standard range of steam locomotives, providing for the restriction of construction of Class 9 2-10-0 heavy freight locomotives to those at present under construction, together with such number already authorised as can immediately be justified by traffic require-

ments and operating economy. Standard Class 8 locomotive to be designed for use on all Regions."

At that time the first 2-10-0 was almost complete in the Erecting Shop at Crewe, but in fact production design of the 2-8-0 was not even initiated, and only two months later in February 1954 the Committee provisionally approved the construction of twenty 2-10-0s for the LMR (plus thirty Class 5 4-6-0s) by *private contractors*. Back in July 1953 the LMR had intimated its desire to put twenty 2-10-0s on the 1955 Programme and the ER forty five likewise, in anticipation of an upturn in coal traffic. However, by this time new construction in BR workshops was badly in arrears due to a national steel shortage, on account of intense industrial demand exceeding supply. It was estimated that by the beginning of 1955 some 280 locomotives already authorised would be outstanding, and so the Railway Executive was urged to investigate the possibility of getting BR Standard steam locomotives built by private contractors if they could guarantee delivery *before* BR workshops. By late 1953 the immediate post-war boom in locomotive construction for export was passing and the British locomotive industry was anxiously seeking orders, having suffered additional disappointment over substantial orders from India going elsewhere. It was, however, a potentially sensitive issue which could cut both ways. Back in 1949 there had been deep resentment at Cowlairs Works in the face of threatened redundancies, when 'just around the corner' NBL was building Thompson B1 4-6-0s.

Enquiries were put out for seventy Class 9F 2-10-0s and for fifty Class 5 4-6-0s. Quotations were received from the North British Locomotive Company in Glasgow, and the Vulcan Foundry at Newton-le-Willows, to supply thirty five 2-10-0s each. NBL quoted £30,058 and Vulcan Foundry £31,268 per locomotive, as against £24,691 by Crewe Works, which had no profit mark up. This hitherto little known fact also explains a cryptic reference in *The Railway Observer* for February 1954 (p.39) that 'it is understood that a batch of C1.5 4-6-0s may be built by R. Stephenson & Co.'. Even the scaled down twenty plus thirty provisionally approved in February 1954 came to nothing, as the tentative 1955 Programme was not put into effect in order to allow the overdue existing programmes to catch up, except for thirty five Class 5 4-6-0s from Derby and Doncaster Works. In the event no BR Standard steam locomotive was built 'outside'. Interestingly however, the machining of the smokebox saddles for the final Swindon batch of 2-10-0s was contracted out, to the Hunslet Engine Company in Leeds.

The first 2-10-0 reached the Western Region at the beginning of February 1954, by which time the WR had successfully reduced its original quota of twenty to only eight, the balance of twelve, including all ten Crosti-boilered 2-10-0s to go instead to the LMR. Soon afterwards it also succeeded in diverting the ten engines on the 1954 Programme to the LMR. Perhaps by way of a piece of industrial psychology, but ostensibly to ease the burden on Crewe Works, in early 1954 the construction of ten 2-10-0s on that year's programme for the Eastern Region was diverted to Swindon. In practice Crewe furnished the cylinders and flanged boiler plates for these as it did for all the 2-10-0s later built at Swindon.

LEADING DIMENSIONS OF PROPOSED BR STANDARD CLASS 8 2–8–0s, November 1953

	LMS 8F	Proposed BR	Proposed BR	BR 9F
	2–8–0	8F 2–8–0 [1]	8F 2–8–0 [2]	2–10–0
Cylinders all x 2	18½″ x 28″	19″ x 28″	A 18¾″ x 28″	20″ x 28″
			B 19¾″ x 28″	
			C 20″ x 28″	
Boiler Pressure	225lb	250lb	A 225lb	250lb
			B 250lb	
			C 250lb	
Max. Boiler dia.	5′ 8⅜″	5′ 8½″	6′ 1″	6′ 1″
Tube Length	12′ 2⅞″	12′ 2⅞″	11′ 7″	15′ 3″
Grate Area ft²	28.7	28.7	41.2	40.2
Driving Wheel dia.	4′ 8½″	5′ 0″	5′ 0″	5′ 0″
Coupled Wheelbase	17′ 3″	17′ 10″	17′ 1″	21′ 8″
Engine Wheelbase	26′ 0″	26′ 4″	25′ 7″	30′ 2″
Max. Axleload	16.0 ton	n/a	17.5 ton	15.5 ton
Adhesion Weight	63.1 ton	n/a	70.0 ton	77.5 ton
Engine Weight	72.1 ton	n/a	80.9 ton	86.7 ton

[1] *BR Headquarters.*
[2] *Derby Development Office.*

Weight diagrams of the alternative (tentatively) proposed BR Standard Class 8 2–8–0s outlined at BR Headquarters (upper) and in Derby Development Office (lower) in November 1953. In the event neither option was taken any further.

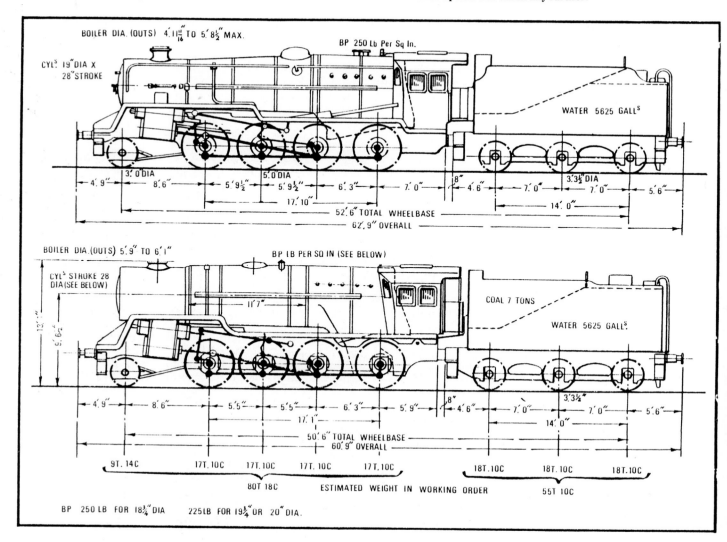

The boiler is lowered onto the frames, the underside of its cladding pre–painted in black gloss, as this region will subsequently be virtually inaccessible. R. Partridge Collection.

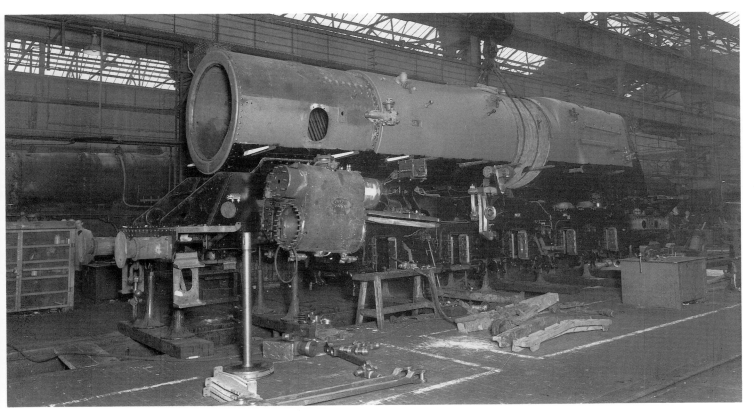

The boiler rests on the frames. R. Partridge Collection.

No.92250 is lifted prior to wheeling; the cab of No.92249, in a slightly more advanced stage of construction, can just be seen to the left. In the autumn of 1958 Crewe Works made a concerted effort to complete its final batch of 2–10–0s before the year end. Five entered service during October alone, and four in early December. R. Partridge Collection.

No.92250 is lowered onto its wheels. On some 9Fs, including No.92099 and the Crostis, the frames were fully wheeled and the motion set up prior to fitting the boiler. R. Partridge Collection.

No.92250 in ghostly primer, poses with some of its builders at Crewe, December 1958.

No.92220 in 'A' Shop at Swindon Works on 21st February 1960, three weeks before its naming ceremony. T.E. Williams Collection, NRM.

BR ANNUAL LOCOMOTIVE BUILDING PROGRAMMES 1951 – 1958

	1951	1952	1953	1954*	1955	1956	1957	1958	Total	
Standard Locos Authorised	159	155	237	138 (186)	35	227	18	30	999	
Cumulative Total (A)	159	314	551	689 (737)	724 (772)	951	969	999	999	
Year actually to traffic:										Cumulative Total (B)
1951	89	—	—	—	—	—	—	—	89	89
1952	70	27	—	—	—	—	—	—	97	186
1953	—	93	30	—	—	—	—	—	123	309
1954	—	21	150	13	—	—	—	—	184	493
1955	—	14	30	82	30	—	—	—	156	649
1956	—	—	5	39	5	80	—	—	129	778
1957	—	—	22	4	—	115	—	—	141	919
1958	—	—	—	—	—	32	—	30	62	981
1959	—	—	—	—	—	—	15	—	15	996
1960	—	—	—	—	—	—	3	—	3	999
Backlog (A–B)	70	128	242	196 (244)	75 (123)	173	50	18		

A total of 186 locomotives was originally authorised on the 1954 Programme, of which 48 were subsequently cancelled.

Scarcely had the BR 2-10-0 made its *début* when the whole question of British Railways' future traction policy was closely examined. There were those who in 1948 had not agreed with the inception of a new range of steam locomotives for a variety of reasons, but by 1954 BR was becoming increasingly unprofitable and the coal problem ever more acute. That year witnessed a further sharp price rise by a fellow nationalised industry in that particular commodity. Hastily forged during late 1954 the British Railways Modernization and Re-Equipment Plan was made public in January 1955, heralding the eventual replacement of steam by diesel and electric traction. Only the following month the 1956 Building Programme was approved, which tabulated no fewer than 106 2-10-0s out of 227 new steam locomotives. However, the latter represented a considerable cut back on the 384 steam locomotives collectively requested. At this time orders were still outstanding for 244 Standard steam locomotives from earlier programmes, and construction orders for 48 engines on the 1954 Programme (in Classes 3,4 and 6) to have been built at Crewe and Swindon were quickly suspended as a result of the Modernization Plan.

It was certainly not anticipated that any further steam locomotives would be approved beyond the 1956 Programme and it was only after considerable heart searching that a total of no fewer than 48 Class 9F 2-10-0s were reluctantly placed on the 1957 *and* 1958 Programmes, and for the Western Region at that! The explanation was simple enough, the oldest Churchward 2-8-0s were now over fifty years old, and the entire 28XX sequence built between 1903 and 1919 would be deemed to be life expired by 1964. At that time no suitable diesel alternative could be envisaged short of resort to multiple working which would have been too costly. It is understood that the North Eastern Region also made a reasoned post-1955 case for 2-10-0s for short-haul coal workings on economic grounds, but was over-ruled in this instance.

Thus eighteen 2-10-0s were authorised in December 1955 on the 1957 Programme, to be built at Swindon Works. Nine months later, in September 1956, no fewer than thirty were ordered from Crewe, on the 1958 Programme, when the

ORIGINAL & ACTUAL DISTRIBUTION OF BR CLASS 9F 2–10–0 BY BUILDING PROGRAMME.

Prog.	Loco Nos.	LMR	ER	WR	NER	SR	Total
				Region			
1953	92000–92029						
	(a)	—	5	20	—	5	30
	(b)	17	5	8	—	—	30
1954	92030–92096						
	(a)	15	35	10	7	—	67
	(b)	25	35	—	7	—	67
1955	(not built)	(20)	—	—	—	—	0
1956	92097–92202	58	45	—	3	—	106
1957	92203–92220	—	—	18	—	—	18
1958	92221–92250	—	—	30	—	—	30
Final total		100	85*	56	10	0	251

Notes:–
(a) = original allocation when authorised.
(b) = actual allocation when built.
* *Owing to regional boundary changes in early 1958 prior to the completion of delivery, Eastern Region Class 9F operational stock never exceeded 55.*

suspended 48 engines on the 1954 Programme were also finally cancelled. Owing to the major turnover at Swindon to diesel hydraulic locomotive construction, delivery of the '1957' engines did not even commence until the completion of all the '1958' engines, and indeed during that year at Crewe.

22

This accounted for the curious anomaly whereby the highest numbered engine, No.92250, the last steam locomotive to be built at Crewe Works, from which it was despatched with ceremony on 16th December, 1958 , was followed well over a year later by No.92220 from Swindon. In anticipation of the latter's unique status as the last steam locomotive to be built by and for British Railways, Western Region staff were invited to suggest a suitable name. *Evening Star* which went back to 1839 on the GWR Broad Gauge, was selected and unveiled with due ceremony on 18th March 1960, with fully lined passenger green livery and a copper capped chimney.

During the construction period building costs steadily increased from almost £24,000 for No.92000 to £33,500 for No.92220. During 1958 when both Crewe and Swindon were simultaneously building 2-10-0s, albeit with differing patterns of tender (which did not seriously affect the issue) the Crewe engines were costed at around £28,300 apiece, as against £30,400 for those from Swindon. The relative boiler costs largely accounted for the difference. Swindon had a reputation for being expensive and Crewe to be cheap, but things were not always quite what they seemed – comparisons could be odious. Some analysis of relative costs at the two works must have been made because whilst it was noted that the overall cost of producing 9F coupling rods was much the same, it became apparent that the forging cost element was noticeably cheaper at Crewe, whilst that of subsequent machining was lower at Swindon. Why not effect a small economy by forging all the rods at Crewe and then machine them at Swindon? This was tried and machining costs rocketed! The simple fact was that Crewe forged to something like ¾in. oversize, as against only ⅛in. by Swindon, who traditionally forged to finer limits and who now had to pare off much more metal!

The tale is also told (from Swindon) that the last thirty Crewe-built 9Fs, produced for the Western Region, on arrival at Swindon for the installation of ATC, in addition immediately had their boilers lifted and refitted. By Swindon standards these were secured *too* firmly to the frames which thereupon suffered some stressing due to thermal expansion of the boilers when in steam. The opening out of a few crucial rivet holes solved the problem. About five years later the construction of some C – C 'Western' Class 2700 HP diesel hydraulic locomotives was subcontracted from Swindon to Crewe which on paper at least appeared to build them more cheaply. The same, not entirely unbiased, source maintains that these required much expensive attention at Swindon before they could be released to traffic!

Close up of the nameplate of EVENING STAR and commemorative plaque. The dimensions of the plaque were 17½″ x 6¼″ x ⅜.

Crewe Works Boiler Shop staff pose in front of the boiler for the last 2–10–0 to be built at Crewe, late 1958. It was not, however, the last 9F boiler to be built there – by three years. NRM

Chapter 5 – Boilers

The decision to build a 2-10-0 in preference to a 2-8-2 necessitated the design of a new boiler, which quite coincidentally was coded BR9. This had been largely schemed out by Frank Carrier at Derby to utilise press blocks already produced for the Class 7 4-6-2 (front tubeplate) and its smaller Class 6 counterpart (firebox) but as with the engine as a whole the production drawings were prepared at Brighton under the direction of R.G. Jarvis.

Spatial limitations with the wide firebox, set above the trailing coupled wheels, dictated that the new boiler should be slightly smaller than that of the Class 7 Pacific. In the latter it had proved possible to achieve remarkably good design ratios, especially as regards free gas area/grate area and firebox volume/grate area factors. On paper those possible with the BR9 were theoretically distinctly inferior, but interestingly subsequent plant tests demonstrated that at moderate coal rates of up to 3000lb/hr (the manual firing limit) the 2-10-0 boiler was actually slightly more efficient than that of the 4-6-2! The ceiling evaporation rate was somewhat less in a similar ratio to the slightly reduced grate area, i.e. 29,000lb/hr as against 31,500lb/hr. The official test report later remarked that 'combustion was as good as can be expected for a boiler with a very shallow firebox.'

A total of 253 BR 9 boilers was built, 241 plus 12 spares. Of these 198 were built at Crewe and 55 at Swindon. Having the blocks Crewe produced the flanged plates for all of them, but in practice much finishing work was still necessary at Swindon, whose boilers were significantly more expensive. Those for the 9Fs were the largest boilers to be assembled there since that one-off *Great Bear* 4-6-2 nearly fifty years earlier, for which nevertheless a full set of press blocks had been made. By way of a curious contrast, no full set of blocks was ever made for the Std. No.8 'Castle'. No fewer than 260 units were made between 1923 and 1961, very largely hand-built.

New locomotive boiler construction ended at both Crewe and Swindon Works during 1961/2, some of Crewe's last boilers being spares for 2-10-0s, which therefore post-dated construction of the engines themselves. These included a single spare for the ten 'Crosti' 2-10-0s in late 1961, originally authorised nearly five years previously. Unlike the ten production BR 12 boilers of 19 , this omitted the preheater beneath, whose value had proved to be minimal (see Chapter 9). Surprisingly the rather complex Crosti boilers were significantly cheaper to build than BR9 boilers constructed at the same time.

Boilers were built in batches for specific batches of new locomotives, but were not necessarily fitted to these in a strict numerical sequence. One interesting situation arose whereby a Crewe spare (1877) was sent to Swindon where it was put onto new 2-10-0 No. 921   being built there. This resulted in boiler 1896 scheduled for No. 92220 effectively becoming a spare. It was sent to Darlington where it was put onto No. 92180 in for heavy repairs, in February 1960.

COMPARATIVE LEADING DIMENSIONS OF BR 9 AND RELATED BOILERS

	BR Cl 6 4–6–2	BR Cl 7 4–6–2	BR Cl 9F 2–10–0	WD/MoS 2–10–0
Boiler type.	BR 2	BR 1	BR 9	BR 11
Boiler pressure.	250lb	250lb	250lb	225lb
Min. boiler diameter.	5′ 4″	5′ 9″	5′ 9″	5′ 7⅛″
Max. boiler diameter.	6′ 1″	6′ 5½″	6′ 1″	5′ 9⅞″
Tube length.	17′ 0″	17′ 0″	15′ 3″	15′ 8″
No./Diameter of flues.	35/5½″	40/5½″	35/5¼″	28/5⅛″
No./Diameter of tubes.	108/2⅛″	136/2⅛″	138/2″	152/1⅞″
Tube heating surface ft².	1878	2264	1836	1759
Firebox heating surface ft².	195	210	179	192*
Evaporative heating surface ft².	2073	2474	2015	1951
Superheater heating surface ft².	628	718	535	423
Grate area ft².	36.0	42.0	40.2	40.0
Free gas area ft².	5.73	6.79	5.45	4.56
Firebox volume ft³.	248	273	213	202
Gas area/grate.	0.159	0.162	0.136	0.113
Firebox vol/grate.	6.89	6.50	5.30	5.02
Empty weight tons.	22.0	24.75	21.4	n/a

*including arch tubes.

BR CLASS 9F 2–10–0 BOILERS (for new locomotives).

Building Programme	Locomotive Nos.	Boiler Nos. (scheduled)	Builder	Boiler Build Dates	Cost per boiler
1953	92000–92019	1128–1147	CREWE	10/53 – 8/54	£5245 (av.)
	92020–92029	1148–1157	CREWE	2/55 – 5/55	£4895*
1954	92030–92086	1410–1466	CREWE	9/54 – 6/56	£5351 (av.)
	92087–92096	1467–1476	SWINDON	5/56 – 2/57	£7124
1956	92097–92177	1644–1724	CREWE	5/56 – 1/58	£6276 (av.)
	92178–92202	1725–1749	SWINDON	6/57 – 10/58	£8299
1957	92203–92220	1879–1896	SWINDON	12/58 – 11/59	£8746
1958	92221–92250	1912–1941	CREWE	1/58 – 11/58	£6415

* BR 12 (Crosti) boilers. The Crosti boiler was originally to be designated BR 9A.

BR CLASS 9F 2–10–0 SPARE BOILERS.

Boiler Number	Spare Boiler Prog.	Date New	Fitted to Loco No.	At	Date
1876	1956	5/57	92012	Darlington	7/57
1877	1956	7/57	92198 *	Swindon	10/58
1901	1957	2/59	92009	Crewe	4/59
1902	1957	2/59	92136	Crewe	1/60
1907	1958	5/59	92015	Crewe	12/59
1908	1958	5/60	92006	Swindon	6/60
1944	1959	6/61	92051	Crewe	6/61
1945	1959	7/61	92072	Crewe	8/61
1946	1959	3/60	92003	Swindon	12/60
1947	1959	4/60	92002	Swindon	11/60
1950	1960	5/62	92093	Crewe	5/62
1951	1960	3/62	92045	Crewe	4/62
1903*	1957	10/61	92024	Crewe	11/61

Note:– All BR 9 spare boilers built at Crewe except Nos. 1946 and 1947 which were built at Swindon.

* BR 12 boiler.

(*opposite top*) **The Crosti pre–heater was designed for both welded and riveted construction. These items were manufactured (in welded form) for BR by Babcock & Wilcox Ltd. – here one is being clad, at Crewe Works. J.G. Click Collection, NRM.**

(*opposite bottom*) **The boiler for a Crosti, prior to the attachment of the cylindrical pre–heater via the brackets already affixed beneath. The BR 12 boiler was noticeably smaller than the BR 9, having only a four–row rather than a five–row superheater.**

The firebox end of a Crosti boiler. The labour intensive nature of steam locomotive boiler construction can be appreciated from this view.

Left-hand view of 92087 with 1F tender.

Chapter 6 – Tenders

The BR 2-10-0s were fitted with no fewer than five patterns of tender, (three of which were closely related), which virtually at a glance identified the Region upon which the engine operated, at least when new.

The basic BR Standard tender was the BR 1, with narrow coal bunker, introduced in 1951. Its tank was designed to a nominal capacity of 5000 gallons, but overflow slots in the pick up equipment limited its capacity to 4250 gallons. On the Britannia Pacifics so fitted and allocated to the Western Region in 1951 water capacity was found to be barely sufficient, and five tenders built for further 4-6-2s in 1952 had capacity increased to the full 5000 gallons and were coded BR 1A. The tenders originally ordered for the first thirty 2-10-0s were originally to have been the BR 1A type. However, the BR 1 and BR 1A tenders were not popular from another point of view. In order to provide a steadier firing platform the cab floor on the 4-6-2s and 4-6-0s, to which they were fitted, was extended over the front of the tender. Despite preliminary wind tunnel tests with models the result was an uncomfortably draughty cab, which led to experiments with rubber and canvas

screens. For future construction it was resolved to return to the old fashioned hinged fall plate attached to the tender. The BR 1G tender was effectively the 5000 gallon BR 1A but equipped with a fall plate. It was fitted to the first ten and last 48 2-10-0s built, all but two of which were stationed on the Western Region, when new.

In June 1951 when the 2-8-2/2-10-0 debate was still taking place, it was envisaged that a number of the new heavy freight engines would be allocated to the Southern Region and they would therefore require a 6000 gallon tender. The early diagrams showed this having a 15ft. wheelbase as against the 14 ft. of the BR1 tender, in order to keep down the weight per foot run to a similar level. It was suggested that the redundant roller bearing axleboxes from the twenty cancelled Manchester – Sheffield Co-Co electrics be utilised on these tenders, and they were indeed designed, in considerable detail, at Derby during 1951/2.

By July 1952 it was decided that the 2-10-0 would not be employed on the Southern but that 6000 gallon tenders should be provided for the Eastern Region engines. In early

The last locomotive tender to be built at Crewe, BR 1G/1561, for No.92250.

The BR 1C tenders of the 9Fs allocated to the LMR, not inappropriately had a certain resemblance to the standard Stanier curved–sided LMS tenders. No.92135, with motion dismantled, at Grimesthorpe shed, Sheffield, April 1958. W.T. Stubbs.

ORIGINAL TENDER ALLOCATIONS TO BR CLASS 9F 2–10–0 LOCOMOTIVES.

Programme	Loco Nos.	Region	Tender type	Tenders Nos.	Originally ordered as.
1953	92000–92007	WR	BR 1G	949–956	BR 1A
–''–	92008–92009	LMR	BR 1G	957–958	BR 1A
–''–	92010–92014	ER	BR 1F	959–963	BR 1A
–''–	92015–92019	LMR	BR 1C	964–968	BR 1A
–''–	92020–92029	LMR	BR 1B	969–978	BR 1A
1954	92030–92044	ER	BR 1F	1119–1133	BR 1C
–''–	92045–92059	LMR	BR 1C	1134–1148	BR 1F
–''–	92060–92066	NER	BR 1B	1149–1155	BR 1C
–''–	92067–92076	ER	BR 1F	1156–1165	—
–''–	92077–92086	LMR	BR 1C	1166–1175	BR 1B
–''–	92087–92096	ER	BR 1F	1176–1185	—
1956	92097–92099	NER	BR 1B	1307–1309	—
–''–	92100–92139	LMR	BR 1C	1310–1349	—
–''–	92140–92149	ER	BR 1F	1350–1359	—
–''–	92150–92164	LMR	BR 1C	1360–1374†	—
–''–	92165–92167	LMR	BR 1K	1375–1377	BR 1C
–''–	92168–92202	ER	BR 1F	1378–1412‡	—
1957	92203–92220	WR	BR 1G	1510–1527	—
1958	92221–92250	WR	BR 1G	1532–1561	—

† Actually 1271, 1361–1371, 1360, 1372–73, see main text.

‡ Actually 1374, 1378–1386, 1388–1412, see main text.

Type	Proposed	BR 1B	BR 1C	BR 1F	BR 1G	BR 1K
Coal capacity tons	7	7	9	7	7	9
Water capacity gals.	6000	4725	4725	5625	5000	4325
Weight full, tons	55·5	51·25	53·25	55·25	52·5	52·35
Weight empty, tons	21·7	23·15	23·15	23·15	23·15	24·65
Max axle load, tons	18·5	17·1	17·75	18·5	18·5	18·1
Wheelbase	15′ 0″	14′ 0″	14′ 0″	14′ 0″	14′ 0″	14′ 0″
Notes	Not built	NER Crosti	LMR	ER	WR	Mech Stoker

1953 the question of BR Standard locomotive tenders as a whole was looked at afresh. For the 2-10-0s a combination of coal and water capacities was examined within the prevailing weight restrictions. It was mooted that arrangements should be made to accommodate if necessary 10 tons of coal together with a coal pusher, but it was not considered that freight working conditions justified this on the 2-10-0s. A nominal 9 ton/5700 gallon combination was determined upon, in a new flat-sided tender tank, developed from the earlier 6000 gallon proposal, to be coded BR 1F. This tender only was fitted to all 85 2-10-0s built for the ER and (without water pick up) to ten Class 5 4-6-0s built for the Southern Region.

Also in 1953 a new, slightly smaller, flat-sided tender tank configuration was designed, to a 4700 gallon nominal capacity.

There were two variants, the BR 1B with 7 ton coal capacity, and BR 1C with 9 ton coal capacity. The former could readily be converted out of the latter, simply by the insertion of a partition plate towards the rear of the coal space.

The BR 1C was fitted to all the hand fired 2-10-0s with conventional boilers built for the London Midland, except for Nos.92008 and 92009, which were originally for the WR. The BR 1B was fitted to the ten Crosti-boilered 2-10-0s, presumably anticipating a reduction in their fuel consumption and to the ten 9Fs built for the NER, where its small allocation was specifically employed on short-haul duties and on which pick up was therefore omitted. The BR 1B/C tender was also fitted to certain Class 4 2-6-0s, Class 4 and 5 4-6-0s and would have been attached to the additional fifteen Class 6 4-6-2s,

1561 from the rear.

31

Nos.72010 – 72024 in the 1954 Building Programme, which were subsequently cancelled.

The BR 1K was directly developed from the BR 1C being provided with the Berkley mechanical stoker, whose engine was accommodated below the shovelling plate, thereby reducing the water capacity from 4725 to 4325 gallons. Although it was originally intended to build five 2-10-0s with stokers, this was subsequently reduced to only three.

Regardless of the letter suffix all eleven variants of the BR 1 tender (including six which were not attached to 2-10-0s) shared the same design of underframe, with 7ft + 7ft wheelbase.

As with the boilers the BR Standard tenders were numbered in blocks within the annual building programme *not* according to their own type, but with regard to the power classification (in descending order, with 4-6-0s preceding the 2-6-0s) of the engines to which they were to be attached. Unlike the boilers the complication of spares did not arise, but the normally well ordered system got into a distinct tangle as far as the 9Fs between Nos.92150 and 92177 were concerned.

In late 1957 the scheduled tender for No.92150, 1C/1360, was appropriated and modified for use behind the solitary BR Standard Class 8 three-cylinder 4-6-2 No.71000, which was in Crewe Works for its first heavy repair at this time. Its new tender was numbered 1J/1528 and its original 1954-built companion 1E/1271 was modified to a 1C type which retained this

serial number and was given to No.92150. A later 1C tender was numbered 1360 and attached to No.92162. The next five engines, 92163 – 92167 were those originally scheduled to be provided with Berkley stokers (see Chapter 10) and these, including the first two, which after all were not so fitted, emerged out of sequence 4/5 months later. Although these were scheduled to receive Nos.1373-7 they in fact received 1372/3/5-7; for some reason 1374 was overlooked. Meanwhile the next sequence with 1F tenders commencing with No.92168 immediately followed on after 92162 and although the former's tender *should* have been numbered 1378 it was in fact numbered (1F)/1377. Some five months later the final stoker engine No.92167 was delivered with tender 1K/1377. As a result No.92168 had its tender replated to 1374 a few days later at Doncaster Shed. The numbering was still one out of phase however and 1387 was never used, like Nos.1529 – 1531, which might also have been intended for the three stoker 1K tenders.

It was not unusual for new boilers to be fitted out of sequence but the fact that *both* the boiler and the tender scheduled for No.92088, the second Swindon-built 9F, were fitted to No.92089, which also entered service four weeks earlier, strongly suggests that the identities of these two engines were inadvertently transposed at an early stage during their construction.

The second 9F built, No.92001. Newly outshopped after a heavy repair, though still allocated to the Western Region and paired with a BR 1F tender at Lapworth, in September 1964. T.E. Williams Collection, NRM.

One converted Crosti, 92024, ended its days with a BR 1F tender. Here it is seen at Birkenhead depot, 27th July 1966. M.R. Stubbs.

Two other converted Crostis, Nos.92021 and 92023, similarly ended up with BR 1G tenders. The latter powers a down freight at Mirfield on 30th April 1966. T.J. Edgington.

92000 on show at Crewe on 21st January 1954. It is accompanied by Webb ex-LNWR 'Cauliflower' 0–6–0 No.58413 which had been condemned a week earlier after a working life of no less than 53 years. Built at Crewe in November 1900 at a cost of £2,178 it had officially run 1,060,5513 miles. No.92000 cost £23,975 (at inflated prices) and would last 11½ years, its total life mileage unrecorded. (No.92001 was credited with almost 132,000 miles by the end of 1962).

Chapter 7 – Trials and Tribulations

In April 1953 it was anticipated that the first 2-10-0 would be completed at Crewe Works during the following August, but it was not until the 20th December that an immaculate black No.92000 was glimpsed standing outside the Paint Shop. It was noted that 'at a quick glance' it 'would almost pass for a Britannia', but it would be nearly six months before a photograph would appear in the popular railway press showing a 2-10-0 operating in revenue earning service.

No.92000 entered traffic on 5th January 1954, three years to the very day after 4-6-2 No.70000 *BRITANNIA* which itself had not been without its teething troubles. Together with Nos.92001, 92001 and 92003, the engine was unveiled to the technical press a fortnight later, and formal portraits of the boldly handsome 92000 in repose were duly published, by which time problems had already begun to manifest themselves...

Whilst *en route* to South Wales Nos.92000-2 spent a few days at Wellingborough shed, but by early February the first six engines had arrived at Ebbw Junction shed, Newport. Almost immediately Nos.92004 and 92005 collided with each other there, whilst the driver of another 9F had a nasty experience when the regulator stuck wide open – fortunately he managed to bring the engine to a halt. No.92001 performed clearance tests on the 8th and 9th February, and several engines were thereafter employed on heavy iron ore trains between Newport and Ebbw Vale. However, by the 23rd they were all out of service and largely remained so for several months, some being noted stored at Gloucester with their dome covers removed.

Almost immediately upon arrival on the Western Region the new 2-10-0s had displayed two alarming characteristics. The first was the slow action of the steam brakes on the engine after a period of inactivity – hence the collision on shed, whilst the other was the tendency of the regulator valve to stick when wide open. In addition the crews felt genuinely intimidated by the new 2-10-0s with their long, large diameter boilers and restricted forward vision, feelings exacerbated by the provision of alien left-hand drive. These same characteristics had contributed to the lukewarm, if not downright hostile reception, on the WR to the BR Class 7 4-6-2 three years earlier, which had by no means been entirely due to any inbred insularity or loyalty to Swindon traditions.

Braking on the engine was provided by two 9¼ in. diameter cylinders fed (originally) by unlagged steam pipes. Subsequent tests with No.92002 on 7th July showed that it took no less than 50 seconds when cold to reach 230lb pressure, compared to only 20 seconds when warm. As a result the bore of the branch pipes was increased and these were lagged. This solved the immediate problem although in 1955

the ER concurred with an observation by the Southern that the steam brake power of the BR Standards in general tended to be insufficient and lower than that of the corresponding regional types. In early 1958 the Eastern Region General Manager, the redoubtable Gerald Fiennes, complained of the inadequate brake power of the 2-10-0s when working Class H loads at 30/35 mph. In response it was pointed out that the 9F was already designed with a brake force percentage at the top end of accepted practice. The possibility of increasing the brake cylinder diameter and altering the leverage ratio of the brake rigging was actively examined but rejected, as this would have provided a braking force in excess of the adhesive weight. Early brake trials on the ER and later on the NER, at normal loadings and speeds, had resulted in over runs of *1000 yards,* the intended stopping distance! In practice the solution was the time-honoured one of marshalling a 'head' of fitted wagons behind the tender in the formation of an otherwise loose coupled train, but doubts persisted as to the braking capacity of the 2-10-0s throughout their six year construction period, even though Riddles had considered this to be a deciding factor over the alternative 2-8-2.

The regulator problem was more quickly solved. At first attempts were made to lubricate the valve with molybdenum disulphide, but the benefits of this persisted for only 7 days and it was therefore impracticable. The cause was recognised as being due to the robust flow of steam through the horizontal regulator valve, pressing this hard down on its seating. To restrict the regulator opening could solve the problem but at the same time inhibit the performance of the locomotive. The original designed maximum opening was 42in², but the experimental reduction of this (by the introduction of a stop) to 34in² on the 'guinea pig' No.92002 on 23rd June did not prove satisfactory. However a further reduction to 24·3in² tried in road tests in South Wales during 22nd/23rd September *did* prove promising.

As a result No.92015, similarly modified, was tested at the Rugby Plant for a fortnight in October 1954, which showed only a minimal increase in pressure drop from ½–1lb in. depending on the steaming rate. As a result a regulator valve similar to that fitted to the BR Class 4 2-6-4T was thereafter specified for the 2-10-0 and installed retrospectively on existing engines.

No.92004 with at least four other 9Fs for company, stands at Newport Ebbw Junction shed on 30th May 1954, whilst the regulator and brake problems of the design were being investigated. T.J. Edgington.

Up to the autumn of 1954 the only regularly active 9Fs were Nos.92008 and 92009 at Wellingborough, which had experienced no regulator problems, whilst the five pilot Eastern region 2-10-0s, Nos.92010-92014 were stored at March, with the exception of No.92013 which underwent performance and efficiency tests at Rugby and between Skipton and Carlisle.

Other minor modifications proved necessary soon after the introduction of the 2-10-0s. The original tender handbrake arrangement needed enhancement to its mechanical efficiency, and yet again the trials involved No.92002, the only active 2-10-0 on the WR prior to late 1954. The high pitched firehole door was deemed to necessitate an anti-glare shield, although these were discarded after about four years. There were some problems with seizure of the firehole doors in 1954 and again in 1958, whilst in July 1956 the LMR reported some cases of heated big ends, which was not experienced elsewhere.

The rather cramped and shallow wide firebox presented some servicing difficulties. Late in 1953 there was considerable discussion as to the location of washout plugs in the throatplate. The water supplies at Annesley were particularly hard and it was later agreed to provide two additional washout plugs in the boiler barrel, ahead of the firebox tubeplate, on each of that depot's 9Fs. Around this same time, early 1959, the LMR began to suppress two firetubes in each of its 9F allocation in order to install two washout plugs in the front tubeplate. One Annesley 2-10-0, No.92088, was experimentally fitted with French TIA *Traitment Integrale Armand* water treatment apparatus, and all the BR 1F tenders were fitted with briquette feeders for on board water softening.

The close proximity of the firebox foundation ring to the trailing coupled wheels resulted in ash accumulating in the ashpan in the narrow space between the two, which it was difficult to dislodge. Side access doors were provided in boilers built for No.92087 onwards which in practice were almost invariably left open, thereby amounting to supplementary dampers.

In early 1961 the North Eastern Region reported that its ten 2-10-0s were all suffering from leaking firebox tubeplates around the flue tubes. It was noted that these were only 1in. thick (copper) whereas ER/NER practice was to make these 1¼in. thick. It is only fair to add that the NER 9Fs were probably consistently worked harder than any of the others and three years later most were out of service with boiler problems – only two were operative in April 1964. By early 1962 the Eastern Region had experienced a number of cases of cracked *front* tubeplates.

Just two years earlier the ER internally discussed the problem of indifferent steaming on the part of its allocation of 34 single-chimney 2-10-0s as against the more recent double chimney engines, of which there were 21, which did not suffer in this way. It was suggested that different blastpipe diameters be tried, but it was conceded that excessive piston ring wear might be the root cause of the problem. Unlike the WR which was currently (1960) beginning to rebuild it early single chimney engines with double exhaust, the ER did not do so, and nor did the LMR, by this time increasingly pre-occupied with ever accelerating dieselisation.

With the final Crosti conversion belatedly entering traffic in mid-1962, it is a curious fact that there was only a single year, 1963, throughout which the *entire* BR 9F 2-10-0 fleet was fully operational.

A very early view of a 9F by a private photographer. 92002 at Swindon on 14th February 1954 inside A Shop for the fitting of ATC. P.J.Kelley.

Original regulator valve design for Class 9F with horizontal grid (left) and the more conventional design (right) substituted after the problems of early 1954.

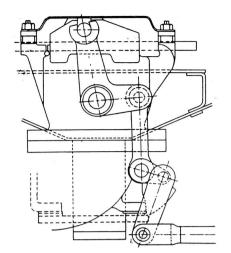
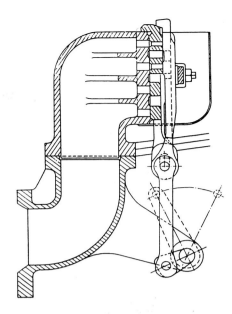

A week later, 92002 is at Swindon again awaiting attention to the regulator problem. Eventually the early Western Region examples were to spend some months in storage before rectification. T.E.Williams collection, NRM.

A clean pair of heels. 92204 recorded at speed south of Birmingham on a freight train, in September 1964. T.E. Williams Collection, NRM.

Still with the stoker fitted but by then largely displaced from the Birmingham – Carlisle work, No.92167 heads a light up freight on Hatton bank, south of Birmingham on 17th February 1962. T.E. Williams Collection, NRM.

Chapter 8 – Ten Coupled Service

The various unpromising events of the winter of 1953/54 well behind them, within four years the 9Fs were well established and highly regarded on four Regions. Around two hundred strong and still increasing, their versatility was truly remarkable. For instance in the summer of 1958 2-10-0s could be encountered hauling heavy iron ore trains in South Wales and in Co. Durham, working London-bound coal trains, handling express passenger trains on the former Great Central main line, *and* banking on the Lickey incline.

There was a certain irony in the open opposition of the Western Region towards the 9Fs before the first examples had been delivered. The duties to which the first eight were allocated, when reluctantly received in early 1954, were those for which the erstwhile GWR had itself seriously considered building a small batch of extremely powerful 2-10-2 tank locomotives about fifteen years previously. In 1938 the huge Richard Thomas steel plant commenced operations at Ebbw Vale, about 900ft. above sea level. Iron ore had to be brought up over the former Monmouthshire Railway line from Newport, which involved an unremitting climb of nearly 20 miles

virtually from sea level, including one short section having a gradient of 1 in 50. The 9Fs were also sometimes employed as bankers, assisting ex-GWR 2-8-2Ts from Rogerstone yard on the outskirts of Newport and up the increasingly bleak valley to the steel works.

After spending the greater part of 1954 out of service whilst the regulator and brake problems were solved, during 1955 No.92000-92007 returned an availability of no less than 87 per cent, which was the highest ever recorded by any BR Standard class on any Region in any year prior to 1959, when such recording for steam locomotives was discontinued. However, the short-haul nature of these arduous duties kept their annual mileage down to 15/16,000 miles, until the arrival of additional 9Fs on the WR during 1958/9 which were particularly deployed on Northamptonshire – South Wales iron ore trains, pushed this figure up substantially.

Following initial trials with No.92037 in July 1955, ten 2-10-0s were built for the North Eastern Region in 1955/6 to work iron ore trains between Tyne Dock and Consett. Over a distance of 22 miles this line also climbed to 900ft. and enjoyed

Only two weeks old, No.92239 heads a down freight at Twyford, 11th October 1958. T.E. Williams Collection, NRM.

gradients even steeper than those in South Wales, i.e. 1 in 35! Two 2-10-0s were generally employed, one fore and one aft, with nine 1951-built 56 ton capacity bogie side tippler wagons and a brake van aggregating nearly 800 tons between them. Iron ore has a high specific gravity and a comparatively short train could nevertheless be very heavy, about half the length of a coal train of similar weight. These workings with their volcanic exhausts must have come closest to replicating in Britain what˙had once been commonplace in the United States, but which was rapidly vanishing there at this very time.

No other British locomotive type became so closely associated with iron ore workings. As early as March 1954 No.92007 was tried on the recently instituted Birkenhead Docks – Shotwick sidings trains which conveyed ore to the Richard Summers plant in the Wirral peninsula. Later Bidston's 9F allocation steadily increased, but after the shed closed in 1963 its stock was transferred to Birkenhead, which by 1965 boasted no fewer than 55 2-10-0s including some Crosti conversions and ex-stoker engines. This substantial stud worked 1000 ton ore trains which were allowed 48 minutes to cover the 12½ miles, which included a gradient of 1 in 100. These spectacular workings ended in early November 1967, just one year after those to Consett.

The original, primary, purpose of the 2-10-0 design was to work heavy coal trains. Early deliveries to the London Midland went to Wellingborough and Toton to handle the Toton – Brent coal traffic. In Midland Railway days this had been worked by 0-6-0s in pairs, which had later prompted the

COMPARISON OF TOTON – BRENT COAL TRAIN WORKINGS 1930/1955.

		1930	1955
Locomotive type		LMS 2–6–0 + 0–6–2 Garratt	BR Class 9F 2–10–0
Loading		1500–1600 tons	800–900 tons
Schedule:		hr min	hr min
Toton	0m	0 – 00	0 – 00
Syston N. Jct	17½ml	0 – 46	0 – 35
Wing Sidings	43¾ml	2 – 16	1 – 08
Wellingborough	67½ml	3 – 36	2 – 15
Leagrave	99¾ml	5 – 01	3 – 07
Brent	126½ml	7 – 11	3 – 58
Average speed	m.p.h	**17·5**	**31·4***

* Overall due to 20 minute stop at Kettering. Actual average running speed was 35 m.p.h.

No.92091 heads a down freight on the former Great Central main line at Charwelton in 1963. T.E. Williams Collection, NRM.

No.92102 passes the isolated and now vanished station at Trent, in the Nottingham – Derby – Leicester triangle, with a train of coal empties on 13th March 1957. J.P. Wilson.

New No.92132 works a down fitted freight at Halesowen Junction, 20th June 1957. T.J. Edgington.

92182 heads northwards out of Peterborough with a short van train, August 1958. J. Davenport.

Region/MPD	Programme				
	1953	1954	1956	1957	1958
LMR					
Wellingborough	92008/9/15–29	92045–9/82–6	92105–8/21–7/54/9/60	—	—
Toton	—	92050–9/77–81	92100–4/9/10/28/53/6/8	—	—
Cricklewood	—	—	92111/2	—	—
Westhouses	—	—	92113–20/50/61/2	—	—
Saltley	—	—	92129–39/51/2/5/65–7	—	—
Kettering	—	—	92163	—	—
Leicester	—	—	92164	—	—
ER					
March	92010–4	92031–3/43/4	—	—	—
New England	—	92030/4–42	92140–9/78–88	—	—
Doncaster	—	92067–76/87–94	92168–77/92–202	—	—
Annesley	—	92095/6	—	—	—
Mexborough	—	—	92189/90	—	—
Darnall	—	—	92191	—	—
WR					
Newport Ebbw Jct.	92000–7	—	—	—	92237–44/8/9
St Phillip's Marsh	—	—	—	92203/13/8/9	—
Plymouth Laira	—	—	—	92208/9	—
Cardiff Canton	—	—	—	92210/4/6/7/20	—
Old Oak Common	—	—	—	92211	92245–7
Banbury	—	—	—	92212/5	92221–30/50
Pontypool Road	—	—	—	—	92237–44/8/9
NER					
Tyne Dock	—	92060–6	92097–9	—	—

No.92096 pilots a W.D. 2–8–0 over the newly opened curve joining the former GWR and SMJ lines at Stratford upon Avon, in 1960. T.E. Williams Collection, NRM.

No.92084 hauls up an iron ore train at Ashton on 11th May 1961. K. Fairey.

An early appearance of a 9F on the GC line. Three years old, No.92013 works an up freight at Bullwell Common, north of Nottingham, on 8th June 1957. J.P. Wilson.

introduction of the unsatisfactory LMS Garratts in order to cut crew costs. Following the 2-10-0s arrival the Garratts were swiftly retired, but the comparison was not strictly a fair one.

In their heyday the Garratts could, and did, with a single fireman power coal trains weighing 1500-1600 tons at around 17½ mph. In February 1955 dynamometer car tests were conducted with 2-10-0s between Toton and Brent in order to determine the appropriate loading with vacuum fitted 16 ton mineral wagons to Class C timings, demanding an overall average speed of 36 mph each way, at a steam rate of 18,500lb per hour. To achieve the latter it was found necessary to reduce the blastpipe diameter from 5⅜ in. to 5¼in. and loads varied from 800 tons (37 wagons plus brake) to 900 tons (41 wagons plus brake). Although 40 wagons could be worked, the frequent signal checks increased the coal consumption near to the manual firing limit and so 37 wagons were deemed to be a reasonable all-weather load. This was thus only half the loading handled by the Garratts, but at about twice their average speed. Oddly, the Garratts were never accorded a power classification.

The two Gresley P1 2-8-2s had been scrapped nearly ten years before the 9Fs took over their former duties between Peterborough and Ferme Park, again with lighter loadings but worked at higher speeds. Both the LMR and ER 9Fs engaged on the London coal runs averaged about 26,000 miles per year which was not a notable increase on the 23,000 miles typically run by an LMS 8F 2-8-0 at this time.

As with the Britannia Pacifics, the ER achieved a significantly higher average annual mileage from its 2-10-0s than any other Region. Rather ironically, the most notable performer in this regard was the curiously remote Nottinghamshire shed at Annesley, which right at the beginning of the classic period, 1958-1964, was transferred from Eastern to London Midland auspices, together with the ex-Great Central main line, to the

respective detriment and betterment of the Regional 9F mileage averages. No.92010 had been lent by March depot to Annesley in early 1956 for trial, following which Nos.92095/96 were sent there new in early 1957. With the arrival of further new 2-10-0s the ER's older 9Fs were then concentrated at Annesley in 1958, where the stud stood thirty strong by the following year. These engines were included in LMR operating stock but operated according to a system experimented with on a small scale by the LNER just prior to World War II, and instituted properly with 2-8-0s in 1947.

The last *major* railway route to be constructed in the British Isles, as late as the 1890s, the GC London Extension involved relatively few junctions and although only double, not quadruple tracked, freight trains could be worked with little fear of repeated signal checks. This underlay the Annesley – Woodford fast loose-coupled freight trains or 'runners' (sometimes known as the 'windcutters') prompted by the desire to achieve better utilization of locomotives and their crews. In the late 1950s the 9Fs were programmed to cover the 66 miles in 2½ hours, including scheduled stops, which demanded running speeds of 50 mph. Turn round times of only one hour were laid down in order to achieve two return trips in one day, and sometimes a third was commenced within a 24 hour period. Given that availabilities of 82-84% were attained, on this basis annual mileages as high as nearly 70,000 might have been anticipated, but the highest figure known to have been achieved by an Annesley 9F was 44,890 (or the equivalent of 340 round trips) by No.92072 during 1959, which nevertheless compared well with the paltry 12,351 miles by No.92047 of Bidston in 1957.

On the LMR 'proper' Saltley engines achieved quite respectable mileages on Carlisle freights, e.g. 44,203 miles by No.92130 in 1960, but taken overall the utilisation of the 9Fs generally was not outstanding and the high point of their all

The substantial allocation of 9Fs to Annesley depot was by no means confined to fast freights to Woodford. Here 92083, in characteristic grime, powers an up express through Charwelton – 24th August 1964. T.E. Williams Collection, NRM.

Following its additional 9F deliveries during 1958/60 the Western Region did not hesitate to use 2–10–0s on express passenger trains during the summer months. Here Crewe–built No.92245 hurries a London – Weston–super–Mare express through Sonning Cutting during the early evening of 25th July 1959. T.E. Williams Collection, NRM.

AVERAGE ANNUAL MILEAGE AND AVAILABILITY OF BR CLASS 9F 2–10–0s & PRE – 1948 2–8–0 CLASSES, BY REGION, 1955–1961.

		1955			1956			1957			1958			1959		1960		1961	
WR	BR Cl.9F 2–10–0	(8)	16,177	87%	(8)	15,199	71%		N/A		(39)	20,599	74%	(54)	27,747	(54)	25,825		N/A	
	GWR 28XX 2–8–0	(167)	28,944	77%	(167)	30,708	81%		N/A		(161)	28,691	78%	(132)	25,788	(118)	27,423		N/A	
ER	BR Cl.9F 2–10–0	(23)	26,737	81%	(46)	26,074	83%		N/A		(55)	35,665	84%	(55)	36,825	(55)	33,154	(55)	32,317	
	LNER O1 2–8–0	(58)	27,685	73%	(58)	26,996	77%		N/A		(30)	21,499	66%	(30)	22,079	(30)	20,946	(30)	20,115	
NER	BR Cl.9F 2–10–0	–	–	–	–	–	–	–	–	–	(10)	21,866	85%	(10)	22,456	(10)	29,664	(10)	24,998	
LMR	BR Cl.9F 2–10–0	(22)	26,122	79%	(51)	24,831	75%	(85)	26,088	79%	(119)	29,548	73%	N/A		(119)	28,984	(119)	28,335	
	BR 'Crosti' 2–10–0	–	–		(10)	21,390	64%	(10)	21,282	64%	(10)	21,458	60%	N/A		(3)	0	(1)	0	
	BR 'Crosti conversion'	–	–	–	–	–	–	–	–	–	–	–	–	–		(7)	19,258	(9)	20,918	
	LMS 8F 2–8–0	(613)	23,067	82%	(603)	22,353	83%	(543)	22,835	84%	(524)	22,699	83%	N/A		(514)	24,442	(514)	23,055	

Note. Availability = 310 − No. of weekdays out of service × 100% all over 310.

Availability was not recorded for steam locomotives after 1958.

In dual harness Nos.92153 and 92156 work a special test train through Wellingborough in March 1959. K. Fairey.

The previous June saw 92153 being led by 92094 on an earlier test working.

AVERAGE MILEAGE BR CLASS 9F 2–10–0s
BETWEEN GENERAL REPAIRS 1957–1960.

	CREWE (LMR)	DARLINGTON (ER/NER)	SWINDON (WR)
1957	—	(4) 79,043	—
1958	(1) 78,823	(1) 90,061	—
1959	(3) 111,561	(8) 79,678	—
1960	(8) 147,995	(12) 129,433	(3) 85,185

Figures in brackets are the numbers of locomotives involved.

too brief era can now be seen to have been around 1959/60.

The deliberate employment of 2-10-0s on passenger trains commenced in early August 1957, with even a 'Crosti' on summer excursions. Their high speed potential had come to light nearly two years earlier in November 1955, when Crosti No.92023 was being road tested in southern Scotland, and it was paced in Nithsdale by a sports car at 80 mph. This fact was first made public via a blurred but recognisable photograph of the engine which appeared not in the railway press but in *The Motor Magazine* for 14th December 1955.

In the summer of 1958 No.92184, then a few months old, touched 90 mph descending Stoke Bank with a passenger train on the East Coast Main Line. At around the same period

No.92093 passes north over Brock water troughs with the newly opened M6 motorway in the background, in the mid–1960s. J. Davenport.

No.92016 passes Oubeck with a Wallerscote – Larbert soda ash train in July 1966. J. Davenport.

No.92164 an LMR engine temporarily transferred from the Midland shed at Leicester to its ex-Great Central counterpart, hauled the down 'Master Cutler' over the 23.4 miles from Leicester to Nottingham Victoria in 23.2 minutes. It covered 17½ miles at an average speed of 77 mph, touching a maximum of 86 mph near Ruddington.

At 90 mph the rotational speed of 8·4 revs/sec was almost equivalent to that attained by *MALLARD* on its record run over the same stretch of track just 20 years earlier. The piston speed, at 2352 ft/min, was actually greater, but not as high as the 2879 ft/min. attained by a Norfolk & Western Railway 4-8-4 at 110 mph (9.0 revs/sec.) in the USA. The 9F and BR Class 7 4-6-2 had almost identical cylinders and motion, and so if the 9F could achieve 90 mph, the 4-6-2 should have been capable of 110 mph, but was in fact never timed above 99 mph. Interestingly, test data showed that despite having *five* coupled axles and plain bearings the 9F displayed a consistently lower internal resistance than the 4-6-2 with three coupled axles and roller bearings throughout. At 50 mph the respective power absorption was 1·85 and 2·4 horsepower per ton of total locomotive weight. A contributory factor here could well have been the exceptionally rigid frame structure of the 2-10-0, whose smooth riding qualities at speed were remarkable, something which certainly could not be said of the 4-6-2.

On the debit side high speed running with the 2-10-0s resulted in excessive wear of their piston and piston valve rings. This was not entirely unexpected, for it had been a major problem with the Standard Class 5 4-6-0s and Class 7 4-6-2s with 6ft. 2in. coupled wheels running at similar speeds. In one extreme, if somewhat artificial instance, 4-6-2 No.70025 required complete renewal of *all* its piston and valve rings

92146 leans to the curve exiting Welwyn North tunnel with northbound empties, July 1959.

No.92033 returns from Annesley to Woodford with a train of empty wagons at Bulwell North Junction in 1961. J.F. Henton.

92143 pulls away from New England yard with an up coal train in August 1958. J. Davenport.

The prototype 9F, 92000, by now fitted with a double chimney, hauls a Bournemouth – Bradford train over the Somerset & Dorset line at Chilcompton on 19th August 1961. During 1962 and briefly during 1963 the last 9F, No.92220, also appeared on this route.

after having run the equivalent of only 3000 miles on the stationary Test Plant at Rugby in 1953. Early in 1959 the LMR issued a Directive forbidding the use of 9Fs on passenger trains except 'in emergency'.

When No.92220 appeared a year later, it was sent brand new to Cardiff Canton, the one Western shed to regard the Britannias with enthusiasm. Come the summer of 1960 *EVENING STAR* was put onto working Cardiff – Paddington express passenger workings including the 'Red Dragon'. A few weeks earlier, on the 29th March 1960 to be precise, No.92204 was tested between Bath and Bournemouth on the Somerset & Dorset line to gauge its suitability for passenger working and proved to be an outstanding success. As a result during the following three summers, 1960, 1961 and 1962, a small stud of 9Fs was temporarily transferred to Bath Green Park shed, including, interestingly, No.92000 and No.92220. In July 1961 the French locomotive connoisseur Baron Vuillet rode the former which by this time had been equipped with a double blastpipe and chimney, and estimated a sustained output of 2240 IHP for 15 minutes beyond Radstock, and a short maximum of no less than 2800 IHP for one minute near Poole. This corresponded to 70 IHP per square foot of grate area, which seems to have been an international ceiling regarding two-cylinder simple expansion locomotives worldwide. French multi-cylinder compound locomotivs appear to have been capable of 100 IHP ft². The *hourly* sustained IHP for the 9F was found to be 2070, compared to 2200 for the Class 7 4-6-2 with its slightly larger boiler.

Apart from inevitable forays over the border from English sheds the 9F 2-10-0s never operated regularly in Scotland as such. They would have been particularly suited to the former Highland main line between Perth and Inverness. In a letter to the writer in May 1962 Riddles indicated that he had had in mind a passenger 4-8-0 for the Scottish Region, which would have been a good mixed traffic locomotive elsewhere.

It will be recalled that back in 1951 a requirement for a small number of 2-10-0s on the Southern Region had been envisaged. These would almost certainly have been employed on the Eastern Division between Dover and Bricklayers Arms, on 800 ton Continental freight trains. Ten years later five 9Fs were transferred from the WR to Eastleigh shed to work 1200 ton oil trains each of which conveyed 100,000 gallons from the Fawley refinery near Southampton to the West Midlands, routed over the Didcot, Newbury and Southampton line. During 1962 the engines averaged 26,000 miles on these duties but by early 1963 were largely redundant, and after a brief spell at Feltham shed, they moved to York, to work ironstone between Northampton and Co. Durham.

Little glamour came the way of the ten Tyne Dock engines on the NER, which occasionally could be spotted well away from their usual stamping grounds. On 18th June 1966 No.92099 was specially cleaned up to work the last passenger train over the 3 mile Alnwick branch in Northumberland. No.92063 powered the last steam worked iron ore train from

No.92151 heads a Sheffield – Llandudno train out of Chester on 26th July 1958. T.J. Edgington.

The first of the North Eastern Region's ten 9Fs, No. 92060, brings an empty iron ore train into Southwick Junction en route from Consett to Tyne Dock.

No.92136 pauses at Salisbury on a Fawley – Bromford Bridge oil train on 17th August 1961. Such jobs involved some of the heaviest trains regularly worked by the 2–10–0s on BR. P. Hutchinson.

A recently delivered 9F with a double chimney, No.92186, heads a down freight at Peterborough in August 1958. J. Davenport.

Brand new No.92049 hauls a WD 2–10–0 and USA 2–8–0 through Rugby on 29th March 1955, after heavy repair at W.G. Bagnall Ltd., Stafford, and en route to the Longmoor Military Railway in Hampshire. J. McCann.

Tyne Dock to Consett on 16th November 1966. By the following year the 9Fs were almost confined to the LMR and a particular route upon which they could be seen almost up to their final demise was the scenic Settle – Carlisle line. One of their specialities since the late 1950s was the Long Meg – Widnes anhydrite workings, which finally ceased with the closure to steam of Kingmoor shed at the end of 1967.

The heaviest trains the 9Fs were called upon to haul in BR days were probably 1200 tons, but over a decade after the end of the steam era on British Railways in August 1968, a privately preserved 2-10-0 considerably bettered this. In September 1982 No.92203 started from a rest a train weighing 2162 tons from Foster Yeoman's quarry at Merehead in Somerset. It is difficult to imagine that this record will ever now be broken, although one should not forget GWR 2-8-0 No.2808's exploit in 1906.

Normally 9Fs received heavy repairs at Crewe for the LMR allocation, Darlington for the ER and NER engines, and Swindon for those on the WR. In practice 9Fs also appear to have received light repairs at almost every BR locomotive works outside Scotland at one time or another, including even Caerphilly, with the major exceptions of Ashford and Brighton. Some of the last heavy overhauls were undertaken at Eastleigh Works during 1964/5. One of the last 2-10-0s to receive routine heavy repairs, including a boiler change, was No.92212 in September 1965.

No.92021 heads an up coal train near Plumtree on 1st August 1955. J.P. Wilson.

A wooden mock-up of the Crosti boiler.

The Crosti 2–10–0s had the highest pitch of boiler centre line above rail of any British locomotive, ¼in. short of 10ft. On these engines the reversing gear had to be modified from that of the 'standard' 9F, with the weigh shaft passing between the main boiler barrel and the pre–heater immediately beneath it. This view was taken during the one and only visit by a BR 2–10–0 (No.92028) to where it was designed, Brighton, in early September 1955. The presence of the pre—heater also required the relocation of the sandboxes outside the main frames. NRM.

Chapter 9 – The Crostis

Having decided in favour of building 2-10-0 heavy goods engines, the Railway Executive in 1951 almost immediately resolved to equip (an initially unspecified) number of these with the Franco-Crosti boiler. Within five years this major project would be regarded as something of a fiasco, but it is important to view this decision sympathetically in a contemporary context. Only a few months earlier, in late 1950, the Government had directed British Railways to reduce its weekly coal consumption by 10,000 tons, which was achieved by curtailing passenger services. It was pointed out that if a large main line locomotive reduced its coal consumption by 1lb per mile, it would achieve a saving of 25 tons *per annum*. The Italian sponsors of the Franco-Crosti boiler claimed fuel savings of up to 20 per cent when compared to conventional boilers. In June 1952 Riddles computed that a 9 per cent annual saving would amount to approximately 100 tons per engine, which would more than cover the additional costs incurred by the ten locomotives which, it had by now been decided, should be so equipped, including royalty fees of up to £800 per boiler.

The principle was simple enough – in a conventional steam locomotive the hot gases passed out of the chimney to waste. The Italian Atillio Franco (d.1936) sought to pass these through a secondary multi-tube boiler, or preheater, in which the feedwater would be heated practically to boiling point prior to injection into the boiler proper. Franco's compatriot, Peiro Crosti, continued to develop the system until the end of the 1950s. Many Italian State Railways (FS) 2-6-0, 2-6-2 and 2-8-0 locomotives of c.1905-1920 vintage were thus modified between 1940 and 1960. Lacking a chimney in the conventional location, but halfway along one side (or both sides!) of the boiler, these were incredibly ugly in a country noted for excellence in other fields of artistic endeavour.

Immediately after World War II the proprietors, S.A. Locomotive A Vapore Franco of Milan actively pushed the idea, getting out schemes in 1947/48 for instance, to fit the Franco-Crosti boiler to a Spanish 4-6-2+2-6-4 Garratt, and an Armstrong Whitworth Caprotti 3-cylinder 4-6-2 in the Argentine. Late in 1950 Henschel in Germany completed two of a final series of 'Kriegslok' Class 52 austerity 2-10-0s with the Crosti

Rear right hand view of a Crosti under construction.

LUBRICATION CHART FOR BR CLASS 9F 2-10-0 FITTED WITH THE CROSTI BOILER.
(right-hand side)

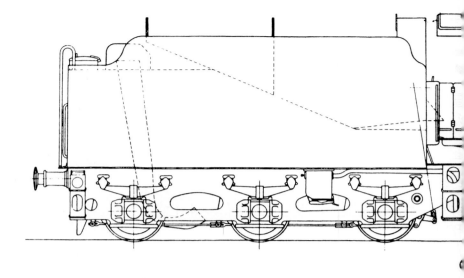

boiler for the German Federal Railways (DB). The Italians never equipped any of their own 2-10-0s with the Franco-Crosti boiler, but it was a wheel arrangement particularly suited to its application. In late 1951 preliminary schemes were worked out in Milan for the forthcoming British Railways 2-10-0. This would have had a separate exhaust on each side of the boiler, and no chimney at all on the smokebox, which carried a large ovoid door serving both itself and the single pre-heater or 'economiser' beneath. To date all Italian conversions had had two preheaters, one on each side of the boiler, and the German engines had these both below the boiler. The restricted British loading gauge permitted the installation of only one, beneath, a pattern later copied by the Italians themselves on 2-8-0s from 1955, which was strictly

speaking known simply as the Crosti boiler.

Production design work at the British end did not commence at Brighton until early 1953, by which time the 'normal' 9F drawings had largely been completed. In addition to the 'Milan' scheme, no fewer than four alternative boiler schemes had been worked up. Two of these, neither of which was adopted, were so-called 'high superheat' schemes aimed at producing final steam temperatures of around 700°F. compared to only c.625°F of the conventional BR 9 boiler at 'normal' output.

In practice it proved possible to permit only limited interchangeability of other major parts with the normal 9F 2-10-0 which itself only enjoyed minimal commonality of parts with the other standard classes. Because of the presence of the

Explanatory diagram of the Crosti boiler, as applied to the BR 2-10-0.

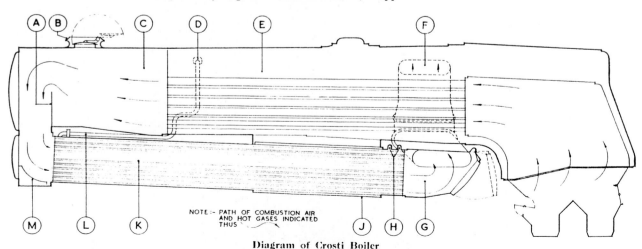

NOTE :- PATH OF COMBUSTION AIR
AND HOT GASES INDICATED
THUS

Diagram of Crosti Boiler

A. Upper deflector	E. Main boiler	J. Exhaust steam jacket
B. Chimney for lighting-up	F. Final chimney (on R.H. side)	K. Preheater
C. Front smokebox	G. Final smokebox	L. Water from preheater to main boiler
D. Clack valves	H. Feed to preheater	M. Lower deflector

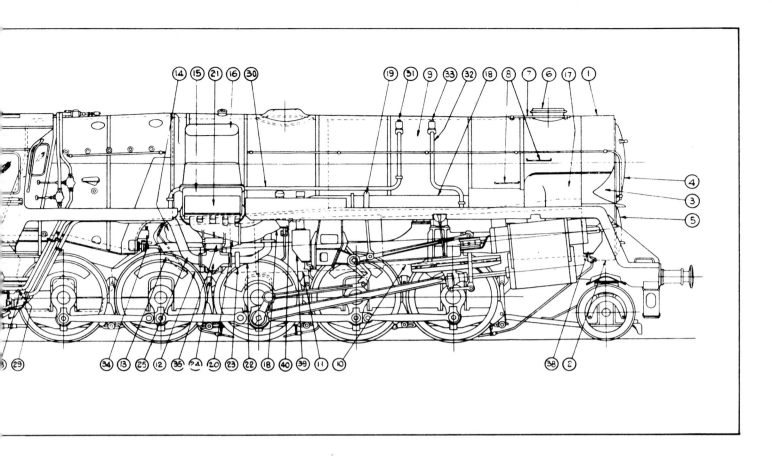

ALTERNATIVE SCHEMES FOR CROSTI BOILER COMPARED TO STANDARD BR 9.

Design Office	Milan	Brighton	Brighton	Brighton	Brighton	Brighton
Scheme	1951	Original 1951	High superheat A	High superheat B	Actual 1955 (BR 12)	BR 9
Boiler pressure	250lb	250lb	250lb	250lb	250lb	250lb
Combustion chamber	No	No	Yes	Yes	Yes	Yes
Barrel:						
minimum diameter	5' 1⅛"	4' 11¹¹⁄₁₆"	4' 11⅝"	4' 11⅝"	4' 11⅝"	5' 9"
maximum diameter	5' 2¼"	5' 0¹³⁄₁₆"	5' 7½"	5' 7½"	5' 7½"	6' 1"
tube length	16' 5"	16' 5"	16' 5"	16' 5"	16' 5"	15' 3"
flues	22 @ 6⅛"	28 @ 5½"	38 @ 5⅛"	38 @ 5⅛"	28 @ 5½"	35 @ 5¼"
tubes	63 @ 2½"	60 @ 2⅜"	45 @ 2⅜"	45 @ 2⅜"	60 @ 2⅜"	138 @ 2"
Superheater:	Schmidt	Bifurcated	Bifurcated	Bifurcated	Bifurcated	Schmidt
elements	1⁹⁄₁₆"	1¼"	1"	1⅛"	1¼"	1⅜"
Preheater:						
diameter	2' 7⅞"	2' 8⅝"	2' 8⅝"	2' 8⅝"	2' 8⅝"	
length	20' 0"	19' 3"	19' 3"	19' 3"	19' 3"	
tubes	108 @ 2"	90 @ 2¼"	90 @ 2¼"	90 @ 2¼"	60 @ 2¼"	
Heating surface ft²:						
tubes	1249	1274	1299	1299	1274	1835
firebox	150	150	158	158	158	195
evaporative	1399	1424	1457	1457	1432	2030
preheater	1186	1078	1078	1078	1078	—
superheater	413	425	422	503	411	535
Grate area	40.2	40.2	40.2	40.2	40.2	40.2
Free gas area:						
boiler	4.54	4.59	5.02	4.80	4.59	5.49
preheater	1.80	2.00	2.00	2.00	2.00	—
Est steam temp.	641°F	669°F	711°F	705°F	669°F	627°F

92024 broadside right.

preheater in the frames between the cylinders, the latter had to be redesigned as regards their exhaust steam ducts. The reversing gear (developed from that of the BR 4-6-2s with 'mangle' wheel and bevel gears) had to be modified, such that the provision of Poultney-type reversing gear, already experimentally fitted to an Ivatt Class 4 2-6-0 was initially considered. A wooden model was constructed to show the proposed boiler arrangement above running board level and, considering the various constraints, Brighton produced a remarkably neat job. No.92028 later duly visited Brighton, to give its designers a sight of the fruit of their labours.

From the outset Brighton determined to mount a chimney in the conventional position on the smokebox if only for lighting up purposes (as had the Germans) and initially expressed concern as to the possible damaging effects of the offset exhaust(s) on glass station platform canopies. It was decided to mount a *single* exhaust on the right hand (fireman's) side, the 'blastpipe' consisting of four in line nozzles of 2½in. diameter (the equivalent of a single nozzle of 5in. diameter) which exhausted through a flattened chimney on

the boiler side. A portion of the exhaust steam from the left hand cylinder was 'bled off' to jacket half of the preheater at the firebox end, where the cold water feed was admitted and the exhaust gases were at their coolest.

Prolonged negotiations were conducted in French with the Italian authorities, culminating in the signing of a legal agreement by both parties in March 1953, some two years before the first engine would eventually appear. The royalty to be paid by BR was to be determined via constant speed tests on the Rugby test plant, at speeds of 20 mph, 30 mph, 40 mph and 50 mph and a modest constant feed water rate of 16,000 lb per hour, in terms of average coal consumption per drawbar horsepower hour, compared to a standard 9F. A maximum royalty of £800 per engine was to be paid for average savings of 18%, reducing *pro rata* to nil if these fell below 12%. No doubt due to mutual linguistic difficulties it later transpired that the Italians assumed the reference locomotive would be operating with its live steam injector, whereas the British had assumed that the Crosti team were aware that it was normal BR practice to employ the *exhaust* steam injector, which

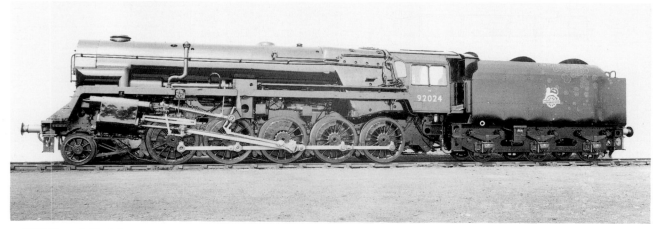

92024 broadside left.

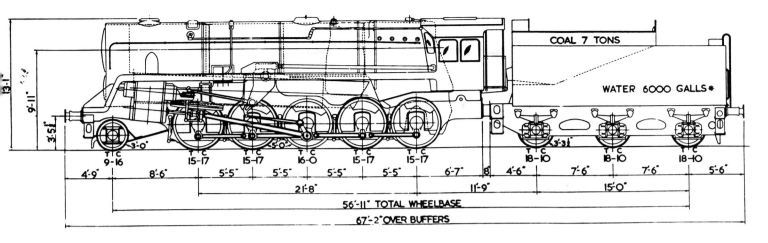

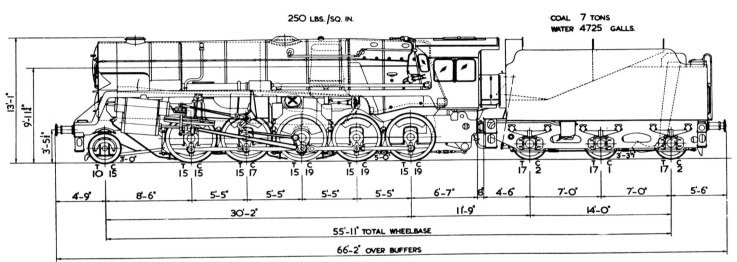

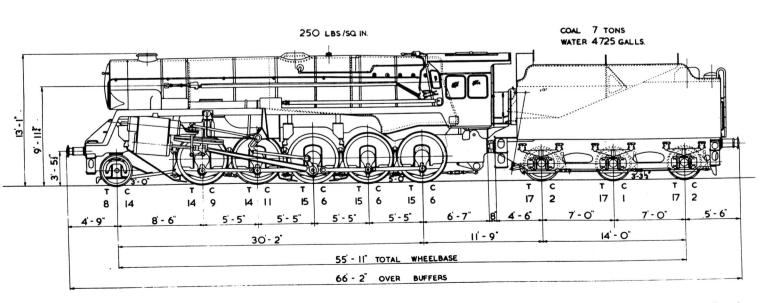

Crosti evolution: (*upper*) Original Brighton scheme for BR Crosti 2–10–0, late 1951. No combustion chamber, smokebox regulator, fluted coupling rods, and 'austerity' chimney. (*centre*) BR Crosti 2–10–0 as built in 1955. (*lower*) BR Crosti 2–10–0 as converted to conventional operation with pre–heater removed, 1959 – 1962.

immediately inflicted a positive disadvantage of around 5% on the Crosti variant.

The original intention to station the Crostis on the Western Region had long been forgotten by the time No.92020 arrived on 5th July 1955 at Wellingborough shed, from which standard 9Fs had already been operating satisfactorily for almost 18 months. Within only a few weeks a feature in *Railway World* for September 1955 drew unfavourable comparisons and voiced the evident dislike of engine crews and operators alike. The reasons could be summarised thus:

(a) Poor steaming

(b) Dirty conditions on the footplate with smoke entering the cab and the right hand front window rapidly sooting up.

(c) The lack of a self-cleaning smokebox.

(d) The preheater tubes also required cleaning out.

It was not surprising that with an effective tube length of 36ft and free gas area reducing from 4·6 to 2·0 ft². there should be initial problems with the draughting. The elected representative, No.92023, had arrived at Rugby plant at the end of May and by mid-July Brighton was redesigning the exhaust arrangements. This was rapidly translated into hardware and rushed to Rugby for fitment. Ferrules were also inserted into the blast nozzles to sharpen the exhaust in order to raise the maximum evaporation rate to the 29,000 lb/hr, achievable by the standard BR 9 boiler.

By late November 1955 all ten Crosti 2-10-0s were back in Crewe Works either awaiting or undergoing modification, several of the new 9Fs for the NE Region being sent brand new to deputise for them at Wellingborough. On their reappearance the stronger blast resulted in the Crosti's coal consumption frequently exceeding *by about one third* the 60/65lb per mile returned by the standard 9Fs. They now

ANNUAL MILEAGE/WEEKDAYS OUT OF SERVICE *OF BR CLASS 9F CROSTI 2–10–0s.

Loco No.	To traffic	1955	1956	1957	1958	1959	In store	Converted
92020	18/5/55	7044	19509	22521	20811	120	4/59–3/61	6/61
O.O.S.		86	135	117	130	—		
92021	18/5/55	10788	18003	18784	21020	266	4/59–4/60	6/60
O.O.S.		51	127	135	141	—		
92022	18/5/55	9789	23561	17922	21397	12005	5/59–3/62	7/62
O.O.S.		34	95	140	117	—		
92023	20/5/55	8675	18145	18010	22483	2407	4/59–6/61	9/61
O.O.S.		120	120	128	99	—		
92024	6/6/55	9981	21767	23646	16443	16157	8/59–1/60	2/60
O.O.S.		34	105	96	159	—		
92025	17/6/55	10962	19784	21361	15376	2	4/59–2/60	4/60
O.O.S.		55	120	104	168	—		
92026	17/6/55	9696	25279	21864	20548	13776	—	9/59
O.O.S.		62	83	106	126	—		
92027	25/6/55	11741	22688	23725	25798	7515	4/59–8/60	10/60
O.O.S.		41	114	92	102	—		
92028	6/7/55	9172	21421	20851	27084	21784	8/59	12/59
O.O.S.		54	106	121	93	—		
92029	8/7/55	5070	23741	24135	23618	8014	6/59–6/60	8/60
O.O.S.		102	95	86	114	—		
Average mileage		9298	21390	21282	21458	8205		
Average weekdays O.O.S.		64	110	113	125	—		

NB. Nos.92008/9/15–9, built 1954 and also stationed at Wellingborough averaged 26,122 miles with 66 weekdays out of service in 1955 and 24,685 miles with 92 weekdays o.o.s. in 1956 prior to transfer elsewhere in 1957.

* Weekdays (Monday – Saturday) out of service not recorded after 1958.

The BR Crostis, although developed from the 'basic' 9F, were the only locomotives in the world to be designed new around the Crosti boiler. Over three years in gestation, their eventual debut almost coincided with the two week 1955 rail strike. Newly in service, 92024 and 92021 are running light together at Elstree on 16th July 1955, returning to Wellingborough and leaving behind a trail of exhaust. P.J. Kelley.

The three phases of the Crostis. No.92021 as newly built, on shed at Nottingham, 1st August 1955. J.P. Wilson.

No. 92027 as modified with redesigned exhaust and side smoke deflector plate, late–1955. J. Davenport.

No.92020 at Wellingborough when newly converted to conventional operation.

carried little smoke deflector plates ahead of their side exhausts, but to little effect. Brighton had considered fitting an inwardly curving extension to the stack.

After a period in service severe corrosion was experienced in the preheater tubes, smokebox and chimney due to the formation of dilute sulphuric acid. This stemmed largely from the sulphur content in the imported Belgian coal and the relatively low temperatures (about 400 °F.) which prevailed in the preheater towards the chimney end. Ironically at this time the Italians were still importing best Welsh steam coal and did not experience this problem, which was also encountered by the Germans. In both Britain and Germany the vulnerable components were renewed in chrome steel. In October 1956 a tentative scheme was prepared to modify the preheater by removing the steam jacket and shortening the tubes by a corresponding amount from 19ft. 3in. to 11ft. 2in. which could have reduced cylinder back pressure and raised gas exit temperatures, the one factor hopefully compensating for the other with a net benefit.

It had become abundantly clear almost immediately at Rugby that the Crosti boiler conferred no material advantage but the tests, which also involved No.92050, were prolonged and conducted with scrupulous fairness over the period June to November 1955 (see Appendix 2). Unperturbed, the Italians suggested that in the light of previous continental experience, under ordinary service conditions a greater fuel economy might be effected. Some impromptu road tests were therefore conducted between Hurlford (Kilmarnock) and Carlisle with each engine immediately after it had completed its stint at Rugby. The LMR No.3 Dynamometer Car (laid down by the LMS c.1938 and finally completed in 1949) was coupled behind the tender followed by about 600 tons of empty passenger stock, worked to schedules which involved steaming, rates of between 14,000 and 20,000 lb per hour.

The constant speed tests at Rugby had suggested that a fuel saving of 4% could be anticipated in favour of the Crosti but in fact this was found to be 7%. The additional bonus of 3% was attributed to the better retention of heat by this boiler whilst standing which thereby gave a higher degree of superheat when starting away. (Conversely it took noticeably longer to

ECONOMY ACHIEVED BY CROSTI 2–10–0 NO. 92023 COMPARED TO NO. 92050.

(A) Actual 1955/ (B) Converted 1957

Steam Rate to Cylinders 16,000lb/hr (Live Steam Injector)

Coal rate lb/hr	Crosti 92023		Standard 92050	
	2018		2162	
	Drawbar Horsepower		Drawbar Horsepower	
Speed	A	B	A	B
20 m.p.h.	862	925	917	976
lb/DBHP hr	2.34	2.18	2.36	2.22
30 m.p.h.	900	933	960	983
lb/DBHP hr	2.42	2.16	2.25	2.20
40 m.p.h.	875	882	939	941
lb/DBHP hr	2.31	2.23	2.30	2.30
50 m.p.h.	827	764	903	839
lb/DBHP hr	2.44	2.64	2.39	2.58
Average	2.33	2.32	2.38	2.32

Comparisons of Crosti v. Standard boiler with live steam or exhaust steam injectors in use.

	Measured	Corrected
	1955	1957
a) Advantage Crosti, both with **live** steam injectors.	− 0.3%	+ 0.5%
b) Advantage Crosti, both with **exhaust** steam injectors.	+ 3.05%	+ 3.35%
c) Crosti with **exhaust** steam injector compared to Standard with **live** steam injector.	+ 8.05%	+ 8.35%

The frames are set up. Note the modified cylinders with outboard exhaust ducts, and special stretcher in between to accommodate the cylindrical pre–heater. R. Partridge Collection.

The virtually completed boiler and pre–heater begin the journey to the erecting shop.

The frames have been wheeled and the motion erected prior to the arrival of the boiler, just approaching. R. Partridge Collection.

raise steam from cold with a Crosti boiler). However, the small increase in overall boiler efficiency was largely counteracted by lower cylinder efficiency, due to the increase in back pressure on the Crosti. This partially explained the quite definitely greater internal resistance of the Crosti which was manifested in the lower drawbar HP, and the fact that under a given set of conditions this engine was always worked at slightly later cut-off than its 'control.' The less rigid frame structure, due to the interposition of the preheater between the cylinders, might also have increased rolling resistance.

The results were so disappointing from the Italian point of view, actually *favouring* the conventional engine in terms of the agreement, that no less than André Chapelon, the eminent French locomotive designer, was called in to analyse the voluminous data. Although complex mathematics was invoked this was no remote intellectual exercise conducted in his Paris home, for Chapelon paid a personal visit to Cricklewood (but not Wellingborough) where, surprisingly, he found that shed staff's and engine crews' only major dislike of the Crosti concerned the unpleasant footplate conditions. This led to him making such practical recommendations in his report as to the installation of sand guns to keep the tubes clean and the incorporation of conventional smoke deflectors and aerodynamic modifications to the tender and coal bunker in order to keep the cabs clear of smoke.

Chapelon could only postulate severe scaling inside the preheater to explain the poor showing of the Crosti boiler, but this seemed unlikely in view of the fact that the engine had been sent brand new to Rugby where it was regularly blown down. His report was delivered two years after the tests, despite which its contents were discussed in depth early in 1958. Almost a year earlier No.92050 had been recalled to Rugby as a part of a (successful) exercise to reconcile the

results obtained from stationary plant with mobile road tests. This was used to adjust the data from Nos.92023 and 92050, again to no practical avail, and so no royalty was paid. Cox recorded that a small *ex-gratia* payment was made to the Italian licensees as a gesture of good faith.

The simple fact was that the standard BR 9 boiler was excellent to start with, the Crosti preheater amounting to a feedwater heater (which its protagonists emphatically stated it wasn't) producing about 5% more steam for a given coal rate with the exhaust steam injector in use. Put another way, for the BR Crosti boiler to have achieved a relative fuel economy of 18 per cent its thermal absorption efficiency would have had to have been 92 per cent, and for a 12 per cent improvement 86 per cent, which in practical terms was frankly impossible at firing rates of 45/50 lb/ft²/hr.

An overall appraisal of the project was made in March 1957 which also reviewed the better results obtained in Italy and Germany. In the former country consistent fuel savings of 22/23% had been obtained, but the point was made that the engines were conversions from early 20th Century designs which left considerable room for improvement. For the two German 2-10-0s of 1950 a fuel economy of 10/12 per cent was claimed, but the weight of the locomotive was increased by no less than 13·7 tons, or 10½% compared to the standard design, whereas the British 'Crosti' variant weighed only 3½ tons or 4 per cent more than the basic design. The German 2-10-0 had shown a lower cylinder efficiency due to the increased back pressure, and in 1954 a DB Class 50 2-10-0 had been rebuilt more on 'British' lines with a single preheater, which displayed an enhanced efficiency, attributed by BR in part to the entirely different (longer and narrower) firebox design.

In May 1958 a senior BR officer recommended that the

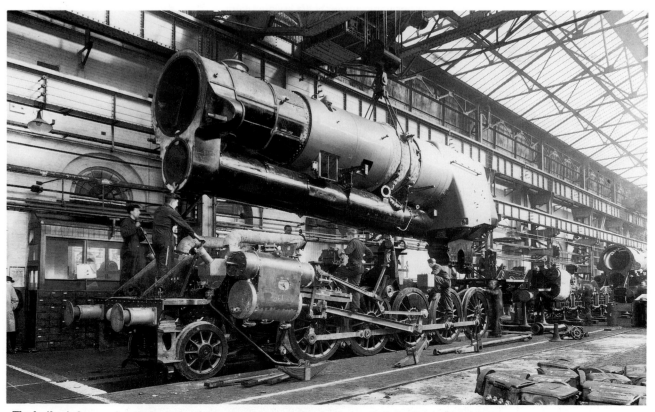

The boiler is lowered onto the frames; the cylindrical pre–heater beneath the boiler is clearly visible.

The boiler is now in position, but the running board, cab, smokebox doors, and some cladding have yet to be fitted. R. Partridge Collection.

The 2–10–0 is now almost complete, and is yet to be painted. R. Partridge Collection.

Close-up of the left side with many components still to be added.

Crostis be transferred away from Wellingborough shed in view of the fact that they were heartily disliked there. He added his regret at the decision in the first place to station them there, for in his experience of thirty years this particular depot was unenterprising and unlikely to have tried from the outset to get the best out of them. He further suggested that they could be employed instead on the briskly run high mileage Annesley – Woodford diagrams, newly under LMR control and which indeed would have been ideal, with relatively few signal checks. The interesting recommendation was also made that the Crostis might be equipped with mechanical stokers, as were currently being fitted to three standard 9Fs, on the grounds that the harder they were worked the greater the relative economy. This reasoning would prove fallacious in the light of subsequent evaluation of the stoker at Rugby (see Chapter 10) which showed this to be distinctly wasteful. It was noted by the Italians that the draughting modifications so far made had been distinctly makeshift and the indefatigable Dr. Crosti now suggested the substitution of a turbine driven fan to give a strong draught with minimum back pressure. Just how this could have been accommodated within the limited space available is not clear, but remarkably the proposal was not immediately rejected out of hand. However, only the following month No.92024 was outshopped after a heavy intermediate repair at Crewe when it was reported that its preheater had been experimentally blanked off and its side chimney removed. By the autumn of 1958 Derby was engaged in producing the necessary drawings to convert the engines to conventional operation involving the complete removal of the preheater.

Most engines had recently gone into storage at Wellingborough before the Crosti era ended, with No.92028 still active in July 1959, just four years and around 800,000 locomotive miles after it had begun. Although the first conversion, No.92026, returned to traffic in September 1959, it was not until July 1962 that all ten had been dealt with, with No.92022 having stood out of use for nearly *three years!* As a consequence of their reduced evaporative capacity the conversions were downrated to Class 8F and they soon became widely dispersed, from Annesley to Birkenhead. As rebuilt, the engines weighed some 6·6 tons less in total, and 4·55 tons less in adhesive weight than as originally constructed.

It is interesting to note that the German Federal Railways in 1958/9 rebuilt a further 24 Class 50 2-10-0s with Crosti boilers on the lines of their solitary 1954 conversion. These were not popular for much the same reasons as their BR counterparts and lasted only about seven years before being retired in the mid-1960s. In the late 1950s a further development of the Crosti boiler was evolved with the hot gases reversing and passing back through the same preheater to a conventional smokebox, where the exhaust arrangements incorporated a Giesl ejector. Other than a single application to a 2-8-0 in Spain in 1959, this system came too late in the day for adoption anywhere even in Italy, though it was also considered for a German Federal 2-8-2.

The German Version. One of the DB Class 50 Crosti conversions of 1958/59. Author's Collection.

The last remaining Crosti 2–10–0, No.92022, awaits conversion at Crewe Works, 8th April 1962. P. Hutchinson.

The cab arrangements of a Crosti 2–10–0. The front windows were rather larger than in a standard 9F, owing to the reduced dimensions of the boiler and firebox. R. Partridge Collection.

Close detail of the exhaust arrangements on the right hand side of a Crosti 2–10–0 as originally built. Note the heavily lagged feedpipe from the pre–heater to the clackbox. R. Partridge Collection.

No.92079, newly equipped with the electric headlight recently removed from the unique former Midland Railway four–cylinder 0–10–0 'Big Bertha' (just withdrawn) coasts back into Bromsgrove with 3F 0–6–0T No.47638, in June 1956. At a later date a rectangular aperture was cut in the front left hand side of the coal bunker – almost certainly unofficially – in order to facilitate coaling operations with the primitive elevator at Bromsgrove – another reason, it is said, why the BR 1G tender was provided. T.E. Williams Collection, NRM.

No.92060, with air pumps fitted to work the Consett iron ore trains, is turned at Tyne Dock in July 1959. It has recently been repainted at Darlington Works, evidenced by the larger than standard cabside numerals.

Chapter 10 – Variations on a Theme

In addition to carrying two types of boiler and sporting no fewer than five patterns of tender, thereby requiring seven different engine diagrams (see Appendix I) there were still further variations on the Class 9F 2-10-0 theme.

Headlight
(No.92079)

For many years Britain's *only* ten-coupled locomotive was the unique four cylinder 0-10-0 built by the Midland Railway at Derby Works in 1919, specifically to bank trains up the two miles of 1 in 38 from Bromsgrove to Blackwell summit, between Birmingham and Gloucester – the Lickey Incline. In the twilight of its existence this was joined at Bromsgrove for a few days during August 1955 by No.92008, probably to test the suitability of a 9F as a potential replacement. On the 7th May 1956 the 0-10-0 left Bromsgrove for the last time for Derby Works, where No.92079 (which had been completed at Crewe a few weeks earlier) was also present. The special electric headlight fitted to the former in 1920, to assist the spotting of its trains in darkness, was transferred to No.92079, which also exchanged its BR 1C tender with the narrow bunker BR 1G tender off No.92009. Half its mileage, after all, would be run in reverse gear, drifting back down the bank. Although remaining at Bromsgrove until 1963, the 2-10-0 lost its headlight about three years earlier.

Air Pumps
(Nos.92060-66 and 92097-99)

Late in 1955 the first seven 2-10-0s for the North Eastern Region, Nos.92060-6 were completed at Crewe but it was some months before they arrived at Tyne Dock. Several were despatched to Wellingborough to 'stand in' for the ten Crostis which were all back in works for modification (see Chapter 9). They were distinguished by a prominent gap in the right hand running board which contained two empty brackets. The engines began to come back north the following April when they put into Crewe Works for the fitting of air pumps to work the side doors of the special vacuum braked 56 ton bogie iron ore tippler wagons, which supplied the Consett ironworks. During 1951/2 five ex-NER three cylinder 0-8-0s (Class Q7) and five Thompson Class 01 2-8-0s had been similarly equipped. The two pumps, which were independent of each other, worked at 85lb/in², one holding the discharge doors closed, whilst the function of the other was to open them when required. Nos.92097-99 were subsequently delivered direct to Tyne Dock with this equipment fitted from new. On all ten 9Fs the pumps were new, unlike those on the Q7s and 01s which were salvaged from ex-WD 2-8-0s purchased by the LNER.

The Giesl–fitted No.92250 heads a tanker train through Birmingham Snow Hill station in April 1964. T.J. Edgington.

Double Chimney
(Nos.92165-67/78/92183-92250)

The original draughting arrangement for the 9F was directly derived from that of the Class 7 4-6-2. Although it had originally been envisaged that the latter would have a double blastpipe and double chimney, the excellent boiler proportions achieved, with generous free gas area and relatively short tubes, meant that a well proportioned single arrangement would suffice. The crucial dimensions were calculated from the formulae developed at Swindon by S.O. Ell and these proved to be 'spot on' in the case of the 4-6-2. Most crucial of all was the blastpipe diameter which in the 2-10-0 was originally specified to be 5⅜in. as in the 4-6-2. However, tests showed it necessary to reduce this to 5¼in., not entirely surprising as Ell's formula incorporated the evaporative heating surface of the boiler, which was appreciably reduced, from 2474 in the 4-6-2 to 2015 ft² in the 2-10-0.

Once the major design work on the BR Standards had been completed Ell turned his attention around 1955 to redetermining the optimal draughting arrangements of a wide variety of pre-1948 and even pre-1923 designs, from Derby 4F 0-6-0s to LNER B17 4-6-0s, many of which (including ex-GWR) had clearly been running for years well below their maximum potential. Even some of the BR Standards, only recently designed, had proved somewhat fickle steamers, the Class 4 4-6-0s in particular, whilst at the same time the quality of available coal continued to decline. Double exhaust arrangements were calculated at Swindon in 1956 not only for the small 4-6-0s but also for the 9F, though the necessary drawings were prepared at Brighton. No.92178, the first of the Swindon batch for the Eastern Region, was thus experimentally turned out in September 1957 and subjected to road and Swindon plant tests. Back pressure was slightly reduced and thereby IHP correspondingly increased for a given coal rate. The blast nozzle diameter of 4in. seemed somewhat arbitrary as it had also been adopted on such disparate types as the solitary three cylinder Class 8 4-6-2 No.71000 and the Class 4 4-6-0 whose boiler proportions differed very considerably, the 9F falling somewhere in between. As the double arrangement boosted maximum DBHP from around 1775 to 1950 at 36 mph it was adopted as standard on all new 2-10-0s from No. 92183 and was fitted to several of the oldest 9Fs on the Western Region, Nos.92000, 92001, 92002, 92005 and 92006, at Swindon between January and November 1960. Neither the LMR nor the ER chose to convert their allocations of single chimney 2-10-0s.

Giesl Oblong Ejector
(No.92250)

The ideal draughting arrangement produces the maximum smokebox vacuum with the minimum back pressure. The so-called Oblong Ejector was developed from first principles in order to try and achieve this by the Austrian locomotive engineer, Dr. Adolph Giesl-Gieslingen, who spent most of the 1930s and 1940s in the United States. Historically the first application of his device, which consisted of several small nozzles discharging into a distinctive longitudinally flattened chimney, was made to a Baltimore & Ohio Railroad 2-8-2 as early as 1948, three years before its first appearance on an Austrian Federal Railways 4-8-0. General development began c.1956 and contacts were made with railway administrations all over the world to try and arouse their interest in adopting the Giesl Ejector. Probably not uninfluenced by the very recent Crosti affair Roland Bond firmly declined, unmoved by

claims that locomotive efficiency would be improved, smoke emission reduced, and that poor quality fuel could be utilised to no disadvantage. Indeed, it could be fine tuned according to the fuel being used.

At this time British Railways with about 17,000 units was the largest single operator of steam locomotives in the world outside Soviet Russia (which despite its vast size could only boast about twice as many) and strong behind-the-scenes lobbying took place in non-technical circles which resulted in the BR Chairman, Sir Brian Robertson, commanding Bond to give the Giesl Ejector a trial.

A preliminary meeting was held at Rugby on 17th February 1959 with Dr. Giesl present, where it was resolved that the official *datum* for the tests should be the specific consumption of Blidworth Grade 2 coal at a steam rate of 18,000lb/hr at an equivalent speed of 40 mph on the Test Plant. It was also proposed to test low grade South Derbyshire coal as was currently purchased by BR as large coal, and as smalls, and a grade not hitherto used by BR of which the National Coal Board had large quantities which it wished to dispose of at the lowest prices. The results would then be converted into monetary savings at current costs which should not attain less than 7½% of the Blidworth standard. This had been computed on the basis of the ejector costing £500 spread over two years, £250 per annum equating to approximately 50 tons of coal, which was 7½% of the average 670 tons a year consumed by 9Fs covering 26,000 miles at 58lb of coal per mile. It was also specified that the ejector should be capable of producing not less than 21,000lb of steam per hour with any grade of coal.

It was originally anticipated that a brand new 2-10-0 would be despatched direct from Swindon to Rugby for the trials, but in early 1959 there was a pause in delivery between the final Crewe 9Fs and the emergence of the final batch from Swindon. In the event the last Crewe-built engine, No.92250 completed at the end of the previous year, was sent and the tests began, with Whitwick and Cossall coal. Preliminary tests were conducted with the original double exhaust still in place, but the Giesl ejector was then fitted. The provisional results were discussed at a further meeting at Rugby on 16th July, at which Dr. Giesl expressed his satisfaction as to the absolute fairness of the conduct of the tests. He conceded that his ejector had not enabled the engine to cope with the low grade small coals, whose consumption had increased to a degree which had completely outweighed the benefit of their lower cost. The NCB for their part had been unable to make these grades more economically attractive by reducing their cost further. Also the ejector had failed to achieve the 21,000lb/hr evaporation rate prescribed.

E.S. Cox as Chairman pointed out that whilst with Blidworth coal the ejector did show a 4 per cent economy under test plant conditions, on the line this improvement was likely to be halved and would therefore become almost negligible. He was thus unwilling to continue with the trials any longer, which in the event terminated on 1st September, bringing steam locomotive testing at Rugby to an end after a mere eleven years. BR was anxious to return the ejector and recoup the original purchase cost, as had originally been agreed by the manufacturers, who now were unwilling to take it back – claiming it to be non-standard. It was eventually agreed that the ejector should remain on the engine for a further year, until July 1960, but in the event it was never removed, staying in place until the end of No.92250's short life.

Despite his disappointment over results with the 2-10-0 Dr. Giesl still tried to interest BR in acquiring a further three ejectors. He particularly had the BR Standard Class 5 4-6-0 in mind and copies of smokebox drawings for these were in-

An unusual view of No.92250 from an elevated position at Rugby Test Plant, again showing the distinctive shape of the Giesl exhaust. J.G. Click Collection, NRM.

(right) **Dr. Giesl–Gieslingen poses by No.92250 fitted with his distinctive Oblong Ejector, minus smoke deflectors and with much associated instrumentation, at Rugby in 1959. J.G. Click Collection, NRM.**

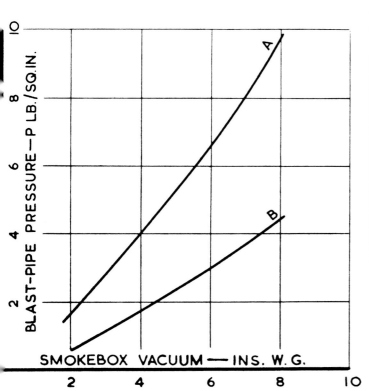

A graph showing the relationship between smokebox vacuum and 'back pressure' for the standard (double) 9F exhaust arrangement (A) and the Giesl Ejector (B), both with Blidworth coal. By comparison the improvement represented by the conventional double arrangement, when compared to the original single arrangement, was relatively slight. Thus at maximum evaporation (30,000lb/hr) respective back pressure values were 12lb (single), 10lb (double) and 4½lb (Giesl).

EXHAUST	STANDARD		GIESL OBLONG EJECTOR		
Coal	Blidworth Grade 2	Blidworth Grade 2	Whitwick large	Whitwick small	Cossall slack
Cost per ton:	£4.40	£4.40	£3.74	£3.40	£2.87
Calorific value (BThU/lb):	12,626	12,626	10,785	10,354	10,116
Firing rate (lb/hr):	2564	2564	3102	4321	7200
Fuel cost/hr:	£5.04	£5.04	£5.18	£6.56	£8.61
Indicated HP:	1245	1297	1267	1267	1267
Cost per HP/hr:	0.40p	0.39p	0.41p	0.52p	0.68p
Relative cost per HP/hr:	0.0	− 2.5%	+ 2.5%	+ 30%	+ 70%
Overall efficiency:	9.8%	10.2%	9.6%	7.2%	4.4%

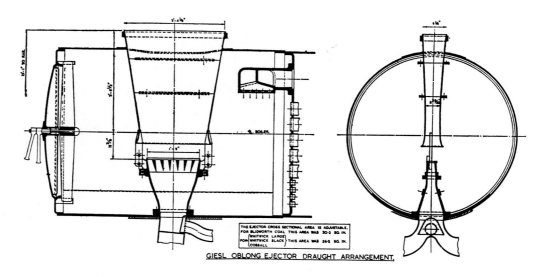

GIESL OBLONG EJECTOR DRAUGHT ARRANGEMENT.

deed forwarded to Vienna even as the Rugby tests were ending. His ultimate dream, however, was to equip a Stratford-based Britannia but yet again he was to be disappointed, even though the 9F tests had at least demonstrated that, compared to the double exhaust his ejector could achieve a given smokebox vacuum at the cost of about half the back pressure.

Berkley Mechanical Stoker (Nos.92165 – 67)

The question of equipping some 2-10-0s with mechanical stokers was first discussed in the late summer of 1956. Like any steam locomotive above Power Class 4 the maximum potential of the 9F design far exceeded that which could be continuously sustained by an average fireman, though the engine was primarily designed for economical performance at moderate combustion rates. The prime intention was to increase the loading of the engines when working Class C freights from 37 to 53 wagons, or from about 900 to 1275 tons. At the same time it was also seen as a means of countering the continuing decline in the quality of available fuel, which by 1957 was even beginning to prompt thoughts of a resort to oil firing, particularly on the Western Region which prepared plans to convert a 'Castle' 4-6-0, and actually so modified an 0-6-0PT. It is also understood that serious consideration was given to equipping some 9Fs for oil burning.

Initially it was envisaged converting ten existing engines in the course of heavy repairs during 1958/9. These would have required new firebox backplates and extensive alterations to the tenders, and therefore, on closer examination (as the 9F was still in active production) it was decided it would be simpler to build five engines new with this feature. This was authorised in March 1957 for Nos.92163-67 to be built at Crewe, but the order was quickly cut to three. Nevertheless all five appeared during March to May 1958, out of sequence even though the first two engines had single chimneys and the three stoker engines double exhausts – the only LMR 9Fs so fitted.

Little account seems to have been taken of the experience of the private British locomotive industry with regard to mechanical stokers, especially of Beyer, Peacock & Co. whose subsidiary actually manufactured the well established American Standard stoker under licence. The more obscure Berkley stoker, as briefly fitted to ex-SR 'Merchant Navy' 4-6-2 No.35005 during 1949/50 was selected and imported from the USA. This increased the cost of each engine by about £2500 and its weight by nearly 2 tons, most of it, according to the official diagram, concentrated on the main driving axle!

The three engines were sent new to Saltley depot in Birmingham, where they were primarily set to work on the 212 mile Water Orton – Carlisle freights, via Derby and Leeds. During the winter of 1958/9 No.92166 underwent extensive evaluation at Rugby, during which it was subjected to extensive *ad hoc* modifications to its firegrate and ashpan, and the twin blast nozzles were reduced from 4in. to 3⅞in. The tests showed the stoker to be uneconomic for a variety of fairly predictable reasons:

1. It permitted high firing rates with consequently reduced thermal efficiency, which was further reduced by;

2. The pulverising action of the screw which generated fines which were ejected unburnt.

3. The stoker itself consumed a quantity of steam which was therefore not available for propulsive purposes.

Although greatly reducing the manual effort required *en route* at least in theory, *on shed* prior to a run it involved two men breaking up the coal to reduce it to 5-6 in. cubes for 2½ hours. The stoker frequently jammed and it was not unknown for more physical effort to be expended trying to unjam it than if the engine had been hand fired throughout (engine crews were changed at Masborough and Skipton). Furthermore the measures of necessity resorted to were potentially highly dangerous! It was also quickly discovered that the screw should have been extended further back into the bunker as the coal at the front quickly became depleted and the fireman at considerable personal risk had to enter to bring the remaining coal forward. The engines could also be hand fired in emergency but the higher pitch of the firehole than standard made this task more irksome. On the Carlisle freights of the three engines No.92166 was always preferred on account of the modifications made to it at Rugby, but British operating conditions with continually fluctuating steam demand and frequent signal checks made mechanical stokers in general difficult to justify. With a grate area of only 40ft² the BR 9F was a comparatively small engine to be so fitted, and it is interesting to note that the much larger and more numerous German Class 44 three cylinder 2-10-0s were always hand fired. In Europe mechanical stokers were only extensively employed in France and Czechoslovakia, mainly on 2-8-2s, 4-8-2s and 2-10-0s. On the huge locomotives in the United States stokers were *de rigueur* but there the hourly manual firing limit was nevertheless reckoned to be 5000lb, as against 3000lb in Britain, and all 425 of the classic Pennsylvania K4s 4-6-2s with 70 square ft. grates were originally built to be hand-fired!

Soon after the appearance of the three stoker 2-10-0s in the summer of 1958 their transfer to Toton was considered, but a year later in August 1959 No.92166 was loaned to the WR for about six months for evaluation on the Ebbw Vale iron ore trains. Ash emission was high, the engine was found to be unsuited to tender first working and there were problems obtaining the necessary grade of coal. In mid-1961 the British Transport Commission decided in principle to remove the stokers and by late that year there was comparatively little work for them at Saltley. No.92167 was sent in May 1962 to

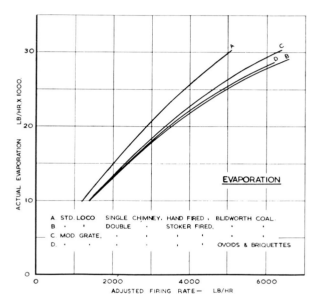

Tyne Dock for trial on the Consett iron ore trains on which it contravened the spirit of the Clean Air Act in a manner legendary even by local standards. Nos.92165/6 likewise with stokers still in place were transferred to Birkenhead in late 1962, but all three engines passed through Crewe Works during December 1962 and January 1963 where the stokers were removed. Of the trio No.92167 had the melancholy distinction of being the last 9F to remain in active BR service, prior to its withdrawal in June 1968.

Stoker–fitted No.92167 brand new at Crewe in May 1958. Its stoker removed, only ten years later it would be the last 9F to remain in service. During the last few weeks of its active existence the trailing sections of the coupling rods were removed and so it effectively ran as a 2–8–2, a curious throwback to the original proposals of 20 years earlier. NRM.

FEATURES OF THE BERKLEY STOKER

Run-of-Mine Coal

The Berkley Stoker takes the hardest run-of-mine coal and crushes it to the proper size without powdering the coal.

Wet or Dry Slack Coal

The Berkley Stoker will handle slack coal, wet or dry.

Cab Room

The Berkley Stoker occupies a minimum amount of space in the cab, having only a riser conduit below the firedoor opening. The stoker control valve, manifold, gauge panel and stoker engine reverse lever are conveniently located in the cab.

Grate Area

The Berkley Stoker does not take up any grate area.

Fire Door

The fire door is in no way obstructed by the Berkley Stoker. It can be used the same as before the stoker was applied. The doors are equipped with *peep holes* permitting observation of the fire without opening doors and causing sudden cooling of the fire, loss of steam and damage to the tubes and firebox sheets.

Lack of Noise

The Berkley Stoker, because of its design and construction, makes *no noise.*

Compactness

The stoker engine is small and compact taking up a minimum amount of space and weighing only 590 lbs. and can be located on locomotive, on tender or rear of the gear box.

Top Deflector

The top deflector of the Berkley Stoker is an effective feature in distributing coal to the back corners of the firebox and in deflecting a large amount of fine coal into the firebed, which would otherwise be lost through the stack. It may be adjusted at the terminal or roundhouse to the position found most effective to perform its function of fine coal deflector and draft shield.

Driving Mechanism

The stoker engine crank case, cylinders and cylindrically shaped crosshead guides are cast integrally, insuring correct alignment throughout the life of the engine. All wearing surfaces are protected by renewable bushings. Its balance is such that there is no vibration throughout its speed range. It is supported on a three point sub-base which insures against strain in the engine base. The engine is thoroughly lubricated by an efficient splash system and requires only *nine quarts* of oil to fill it. Leakage is guarded against by oil seals.

Long Life and Low Maintenance Cost

The Berkley Stoker is *simple* in *design* with all wearing parts made of special steel; the gears are heat treated, properly lubricated and sealed with oil seals, which insure long life with a minimum of maintenance.

The manufacturer's claims for the Berkley stoker.

BERKLEY STOKER ARRANGEMENT AND LUBRICATION

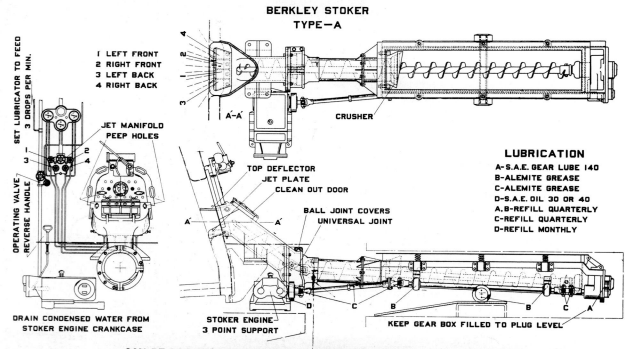

CAN BE LOCATED ON LOCOMOTIVE, TENDER OR REAR OF GEAR BOX

An explanatory diagram of the Berkley mechanical stoker.

Cab view of a 9F 2–10–0 with mechanical stoker. The engine could still be hand fired, as indeed sometimes proved necessary, but the fire-hole was pitched higher than in a standard 9F. *(below)* Front of the BR 1K tender for one of the three stoker–fired 2–10–0s showing the stoker engine, lower right, and feed screw. R. Partridge Collection.

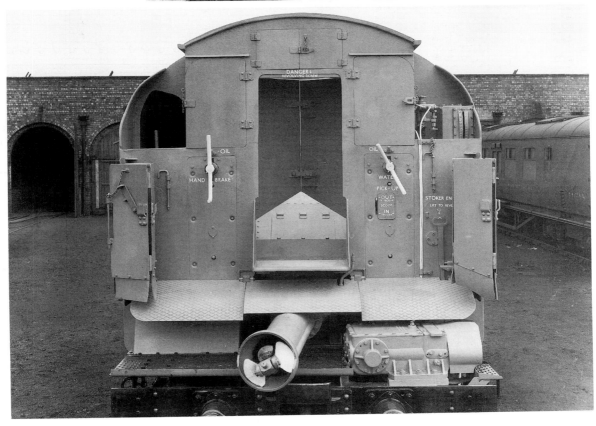

March 1968 – 92127 waits amongst the debris of previous occupants of Buttigieg's scrapyard at Newport in South Wales. Withdrawn in September 1967, the former Kingmoor engine had arrived in Newport by the following November to await its fate. N.E. Preedy.

Chapter 11 – Demise

No *major* class of British steam locomotive built in such substantial numbers enjoyed such a brief existence as the 9F, which averaged only *one fifth* of its theoretical 45 year economic life. In practice this ranged from a mere five years for No.92220 to just over fourteen years achieved by No.92004. The comparatively fleeting existence of the BR Standard 2-10-0s more than anything else highlighted the revolution wrought by the BR Modernisation Plan from 1955 onwards. This was made public just one year after the unveiling of the 9F and whilst it acknowledged that 'in the past the steam locomotive had served the railways well' it affirmed 'that many factors combine to indicate that the end of the steam era is now at hand'.

The steam locomotive in Great Britain undoubtedly attained its apogee on the eve of World War II by which time a high degree of technical refinement and reliability had been achieved and good quality coal was still readily available at low cost, which it never would be again after 1939. Soon the steam locomotive came to be regarded as a necessary evil whose eventual total elimination was regarded as an ultimate if exceedingly remote goal. As early as December 1942, in a report anticipating post-war steam locomotive development on the LMS, E.S. Cox observed that 'it is difficult to see complete elimination of the steam locomotive in this country in the next twenty years even under the most drastic decisions'.

Such 'drastic decisions' began to be made twelve years later in late 1954 'in response to the growing shortage of suitable large coal, the insistent demand for a reduction in air pollution, and for greater cleanliness in trains'. Other inescapable factors were 'the hard manual labour for such tasks as the firing, cleaning, and servicing of (steam) locomotives (which) was not only unattractive but also represented an inherently wasteful use of labour resources'. It was calculated at that time that if no further steam locomotives were built and those already in being were allowed to depreciate in a normal manner, they would be eliminated in 40 years at an average scrapping rate of 466 units per annum. One faction urged a target of twenty years with 1300 per annum being condemned during the first five years, and 800 per year during the remaining fifteen years. It was thought likely that the reality lay

92003 was an early candidate for withdrawal being condemned in March 1965. This photograph taken at Swindon shed in November 1958 shows it awaiting works with accident damage. T.E.Williams collection NRM.

somewhere between these two extremes with some 5,000 steam locomotives still remaining in service in 1975, and their final elimination due in 1985. A comprehensive review of future BR workshop requirements compiled in early 1959 conceded that the steam locomotive might not totally vanish from British Railways until 1990!

Nevertheless, even as the final batch of 2-10-0s emerged from Swindon the first significant inroad began to be made into the BR steam fleet, including the condemnation of a WR 0-6-0PT which had been built only *four years* earlier, and ex-LNER 4-6-2s began their journey to the scrapyard. Even so, the almost cataclysmic changes on British Railways during the approaching 1960s when route mileage would be slashed from 18,000 to 12,000 and 14,000 steam locomotives would be eliminated in barely eight years, were scarcely even dreamt of. Thus Brian Perren concluded an article on the Great Central line in *Trains Illustrated* for December 1960 with what proved to be the remarkably *un*prophetic words 'general dieselisation of the line is planned but its many Class 9 2-10-0s are all of comparatively recent construction and it seems unlikely that they will be superseded for many years'. In fact the Annesley – Woodford freight services ceased only 4½ years later, in mid-June 1965, just one year after several six year old 9Fs had been condemned elsewhere. Britain's last main line to be built was closed almost in its entirety a mere fifteen months later, as an early casualty of Dr. Richard Beeching's 'Reshaping

REGION	LMR	ER	WR	NER	Total
No. built for:–	100	85	56	10	251
No. withdrawn by:–	144	55	29	23	251

of British Railways' plan published in March 1963. The so-called Beeching Report laid down no timetable for the elimination of steam traction but already an embargo was in force concerning any further capital expenditure upon it. By this time an unspoken target was 1972, but in early 1965 it was announced that it was intended to eliminate steam working on BR by 1968 if not earlier. By the end of 1962 on BR diesel worked mileage exceeded steam, average fuel plus crew costs amounting to only 14p per mile, compared to 41p by steam.

A major slaughter had already taken place during 1962 with around 2,900 steam locomotives condemned, including some BR Standards, but the general plan was to go for a phased elimination at the rate of two Regions per year during 1965, 1966 and 1967. Ironically the first two Regions thus scheduled, the Eastern and the Western, had been the recipients of the most recently built 2-10-0s. Technically the first 9F to be condemned was No.92223 on the WR in February 1964, then with a mere 90,000 miles to its credit, on account of the poor condition of its cylinders. In the event it was subsequently reprieved, repaired and transferred to the LMR where it remained active for another four years. At the end of May 1964 the ER condemned no fewer than seven 9Fs, six of them of 1957/8 build. In fact not one of the 92178 – 92202 sequence enjoyed a reprieve through transfer elsewhere, usually being condemned where it stood upon closure of its depot. Many of the older 2-10-0s built for the Eastern Region were concentrated at Annesley. Since early 1958 this depot had come under the control of the LMR, which transferred its 9Fs elsewhere prior to closure of the shed in late 1965. On this basis it might broadly be said that the earliest and latest ER 2-10-0s respectively represented the best and worst return on capital expenditure of the 9Fs as a whole, the Crostis excepted.

Steam working was eliminated on the Eastern Region in April 1966, just four months after this had been effected (on schedule) on the Western, as from 1st January. As a consequence many of the 92203 – 92250 sequence enjoyed but brief working lives, none more so than No.92220 which was withdrawn at the end of March 1965, almost five years to the day after it had entered service. Several were transferred to the LMR and NER and no fewer than 125, or half those built, were still in operating stock at the beginning of 1967. This included nine newly transferred by the NER from York to Wakefield; the last three of these were retired in early June 1967, coincident with the closure of Wakefield mpd, which had come within the NER in 1956. The closure of Birkenhead shed at the beginning of November 1967 eliminated 28 9Fs at a stroke, leaving allocations only at Kingmoor, Speke Junction and Carnforth. The former closed at the year's end, leaving seventeen engines at Carnforth and Speke to greet 1968. The last of

The third of the stoker 2–10–0s, 92167, heads a heavy up mixed freight near Long Preston, south of Settle. This was the last 9F to be withdrawn albeit as a 2–8–2. J. Davenport.

76

SUMMARY OF BR CLASS 9F 2–10–0 LOCOMOTIVES IN PRESERVATION.

Loco No.	Built	Withdrawn from service	Normal location
92134	Crewe 5/57	12/66	North Yorkshire Moors Rly (when restored).
92203	Swindon 4/59	11/67	East Somerset Rly, Cranmore.
92207	Swindon 5/59	12/64	East Lancashire Rly, Bury.
92212	Swindon 9/59	1/68	Great Central Rly, Loughborough.
92214	Swindon 10/59	8/65	Midland Rly Centre, Butterley.
92219	Swindon 1/60	8/65	Midland Rly Centre, Butterley.
92220	Swindon 3/60	3/65	National Rly Museum, York.
92240	Crewe 10/58	8/65	Bluebell Rly, Sheffield Park.
92245	Crewe 11/58	12/64	Wales Railway Centre, Cardiff.

Looking like a condemned locomotive, 92225 was simply awaiting works at Swindon when captured on film in May 1964 – the month when the Eastern Region withdrew the first examples of the class no less than seven in one fell swoop. J.Davenport.

these, No.92167, was condemned at Carnforth at the end of June, latterly running with the trailing coupling rod sections removed, making it a 2-8-2!

The obvious candidates *if* there had ever been the intention to create a strategic reserve of steam locomotives, all but ten 2-10-0s had been reduced to scrap by private breakers by the end of 1968. Uniquely No.92220 had been scheduled for eventual official preservation from the moment it had been built. However, at the time of its early withdrawal it had suffered minor front end damage and BR demurred as to the cost of the necessary repairs. It is understood that secret negotiations took place concerning possible private purchase but in the end *EVENING STAR* was repaired and fully repainted at *Crewe* Works during 1967, to remain in the National Collection. After a period of storage it was transferred to the then new National Railway Museum at York for the latter's opening in September 1975 and has normally resided there ever since. Nevertheless it has operated in many parts of the country on occasion, particularly over the Settle – Carlisle line, which it almost certainly never traversed during its all too brief BR working life. No.92203 which worked the last John Summers iron ore train on 6th November 1967, was sub-

sequently purchased by the artist David Shepherd, who later named it *BLACK PRINCE*.

Eight 9Fs then languished at Woodham's scrapyard at Barry in South Wales (five of them early withdrawals from 1964/5) until 1980, when No.92085 was cut up. Remarkably, however, between then and 1988 the other seven have all been rescued by preservation groups. Like Nos.92203 and 92220 six are from the final 48 engines with double chimneys and BR 1G tenders built at Crewe and Swindon during 1958-60 for the Western Region. In September 1990 the Bluebell Railway completed the restoration of No.92240 which, as it had required a new tender, had this deliberately built to the BR 1B pattern. It is surely a matter for some regret that no example of a BR 1F tender survives in preservation. The only remaining 9F with a single chimney, No.92134, is gradually being restored for the North Yorkshire Moors Railway.

No.92245 was removed from Barry in 1988 having spent no less than *twenty three* years there, compared to a BR working life of merely six years! Inevitably time and the elements have taken a heavy toll and the restoration work required will be truly enormous, a far cry indeed from the days when Crewe Works was completing at least one new 2-10-0 every week.

At 90,000lb, even with limited maximum (50 per cent) cut-off, the Pennsylvania Railroad Class I1s ranked as the world's most powerful 2–10–0. With wide Belpaire fireboxes they had a slight passing resemblance to the BR 9F. (The three–bar slidebars of the BR engines were directly derived from PRR practice via Doncaster.) The Pennsy 2–10–0s sported an even wider variety of tender types than did their BR counterparts, running on two, four, six and even eight–wheeled trucks. Introduced nearly forty years before the British Railways 9F, it was likewise evolved from an earlier 4–6–2, via a 2–8–2. P. Ransome–Wallis Collection, NRM.

Chapter 12 – The 2–10–0 Abroad

The World's first 2-10-0, or Decapod, was built experimentally in the United States as early as 1867 by the Lehigh Valley Railroad, only one year after that concern pioneered the 2-8-0. The 2-8-0 was the most prolific wheel arrangement ever employed in the USA, with some 31,000 being built and it sufficed until the early twentieth century, such that the 2-10-0 received remarkably little adoption there, with one major exception. The biggest user of 2-8-0s was the huge Pennsylvania Railroad which had no fewer than 3,335 on its books as late as 1924, eight years after it had taken delivery of its last new example in 1916, when a prototype 2-10-0 (Class I1s) had also been built.

The PRR made a speciality of developing locomotives on wheel arrangements which its contemporaries regarded as obsolete, and the 2-10-0 was directly developed from its Class L1 2-8-2 of 1914, which was the highly interchangeable freight equivalent of the celebrated Class K4s passenger 4-6-2, designed in tandem. This, remarkably, foreshadowed the evolution of the BR 9F four decades later, and size apart there was something of a passing resemblance in that (unusually in the USA) the PRR employed the Belpaire firebox. During 1922-23

a further 597 engines were built, no fewer than 475 by the Baldwin Locomotive Works which constituted the largest single locomotive order ever placed by a privately owned railway in peacetime. One of these engines brought steam operation on the Pennsylvania to an end in November 1957.

With 90,000lb tractive effort the PRR I1s was the most powerful 2-10-0 ever built, but in terms of sheer physical bulk it was eclipsed by the Western Maryland I2 with an axleload of 35 tons, of which twenty were built by BLW in 1927. These had particularly large tenders, almost as long and almost as heavy as the engines themselves. Four more engines were built to the same drawings with smaller tenders having booster trucks, for the Lehigh & New England Railroad in 1929-31.

Far more 2-10-0s were built in the USA for export, than for home consumption, particularly for Russia during both World Wars. In addition to importing 3,000 2-10-0s the Russians themselves built at least 10,000 of this type between 1934 and 1954.

The first 2-10-0s to be built for service in Europe appeared in Austria in 1906, which was followed by France in 1909,

The largest and most powerful steam locomotives in regular production in Europe were the German three–cylinder Class 44 2–10–0s, the last of which remained in active service in West Germany until 1977. P. Ransome–Wallis Collection, NRM.

Belgium in 1910, Switzerland in 1913, Germany in 1915 and Italy in 1922. Ultimately around 15,000 2-10-0s were built to German designs, nearly half of them during World War II, some in occupied countries. The largest was the Deutsche Reichsbahn three cylinder Class 44 introduced in 1926, which also ranked as the largest and most powerful steam locomotive to have been built in *substantial* numbers for service in Europe. The lightweight two cylinder wartime Austerity Class 52 'Kreigslok' saw widespread service during and after World War II from Norway to Bulgaria, nearly 7000 having been built. Nearly one thousand 2-10-0s were built each in Poland and Czechoslovakia, to indigenous designs, some before 1939.

Four cylinder compound 2-10-0s were built in Switzerland and France, of which the most elegant were the Nord engines adopted as a standard design by the SNCF (Class 150P) and built until as late as 1951. These had long narrow Belpaire fireboxes and mechanical stokers and were sometimes used on passenger trains.

Probably the most outstanding European 2-10-0 design was the Czech 556.0 Class built by Skoda from 1952. This combined the best features of French and German practice, incorporating double Kylchap exhaust and mechanical stokers, and was reputably capable of a sustained 3000 IHP. No.556.510, the Czech equivalent of *EVENING STAR* has been preserved. As late as 1957 new 2-10-0s were still being built in Britain, Czechoslovakia, East Germany, Poland and Roumania.

Unknown in Australia, the 2-10-0 was rare in Africa, being confined to Algeria and the Belgian Congo, and in South America (Brazil, Argentina and Uruguay). It was almost only found on the 4ft. 8½in. and 5ft. gauges. Those for Argentina and the thirty massive four cylinder engines built by NBL in 1919 for the Great Indian Peninsula Railway were exceptional in that they ran on the 5ft. 6in. gauge. Conversely the 2-10-0 seems rarely to have been built for the narrow gauge, only those for the Belgian Congo (3ft. 6in.) being known. The 2-10-0 rarely resulted from rebuilding, but a handful on the Canadian Pacific were transformed from short-lived 0-6-6-0 Mallets and a small class in Norway was reconstructed from 0-10-0s.

2-10-0s were built in about fourteen countries for their own use and for export to an equal number of others. The Baldwin Locomotive Works built them for Brazil (5ft. 3in. gauge) as early as 1885 and Robert Stephenson & Co. for Argentina in 1905. At a conservative estimate something like 33,000 2-10-0s were built worldwide, or around 5% of the estimated 650,000 steam locomotives constructed. The final examples were a pair of German design assembled in Turkey in 1961, i.e. nearly one hundred years after the first was built.

Arguably the most sophisticated 2–10–0 was the Czech CSD Class 556.0, built 1952–57. Author's Collection.

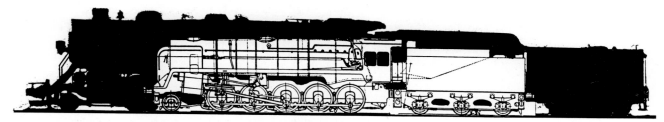

A comparison between the BR 9F and the largest 2–10–0, the Western Maryland I2, built by the Baldwin Locomotive Works in 1927. Its tender was almost as long and almost as heavy as the locomotive!

COMPARATIVE LEADING DIMENSIONS OF WORLDWIDE 2–10–0 LOCOMOTIVE DESIGNS.

Country.	CONGO	UK	FRANCE	GERMANY	CZECH	USA	USA	USSR	INDIA
Gauge.	3' 6"	4' 8½"	4' 8½"	4' 8½"	4' 8½"	4' 8½"	4' 8½"	5' 0"	5' 6"
Railway.	CR	BR	SNCF	DR	CSD	PRR	WMR	SZ	GIPR
Class.	—	9F	150P	44	556.0	I1s	I2	L	N1
Cylinders No.	2	2	2HP 19.3x26.8"	3	2	2	2	2	4
Cylinder size.	22¾" x 21¾"	20" x 28"	2LP 25.2" x 27.6"	21.7" x 26"	21.7" x 26"	30½" x 32"	30" x 32"	25.5" x 31.5"	20" x 26"
Boiler pressure lb/in².	205	250	256	228	256	250	240	198	160
Evaporative H.S. ft².	1883	2015	2084	2562	2163	4590	4574	2420	2968
Superheater ft².	602	535	656	1076	681	1634	1248	1220	617
Grate area ft².	47.0	40.2	38.0	48.9	46.7	69.9	104.5	64.5	45.0
Adhesion weight tons.	72.0	77.5	89.2	93.7	82.7	157.4	172.7	90.0	94.5
Engine weight tons.	80.3	86.7	103.5	108.4	97.4	172.4	187.2	102.0	108.0
Driving wheel dia.	3' 3¾"	5' 0"	5' 1"	4' 7"	4' 7"	5' 2"	5' 1"	4' 11"	4' 8½"

The world's ultimate 2–10–0 design was the East German Class 50.40, built between 1956 and 1960. Author's Collection.

Appendices

Appendix One

BR Standard Steam Locomotive Diagrams

In March 1952 a simple classification system was devised for BR Standard steam locomotive diagrams. These were prefixed by SL (Standard Locomotive) which preceded a code indicating power class and wheel arrangement. The latter was based on the former LNER system except that the long redundant 'R' (originally 0-8-2) was appropriated for the 2-10-0; additionally 'T' indicated a tank engine;
i.e. A = 4-6-2, B = 4-6-0, K = 2-6-0,
LT = 2-6-4T, R = 2-10-0 and VT = 2-6-2T.

The final element consisted of a variant number which particularly concerned tender type. A total of seven diagrams were issued for the Class 9F 2-10-0s as follows:

The uniform coupled axle loading of 15T 10C shown on the 'basic' 2–10–0 diagrams (1, 3, 4 & 5) represented an *objective* rather than reality. When No. 92000 was weighed brand new at Gorton in January 1954, individual loadings were found to vary between 15T 3C on no. 2 axle, to 15T 18C on no. 4 axle. When the same engine was weighed at Swindon the following month the no. 5 axle was initially found to be carrying 18T 3C!

Code	Tender type	Note	First example built
SL/9R/1	BR 1G	(WR allocation)	January 1954
SL/9R/2	BR 1B	Crosti boiler	May 1955
SL/9R/3	BR 1F	(ER allocation)	May 1954
SL/9R/4	BR 1C	(LMR allocation)	September 1954
SL/9R/5	BR 1B	(NER allocation)	November 1955
SL/9R/6	BR 1K	Mechanical stoker & double chimney	April 1958
SL/9R/7	BR 1B	'Crosti conversion	September 1959

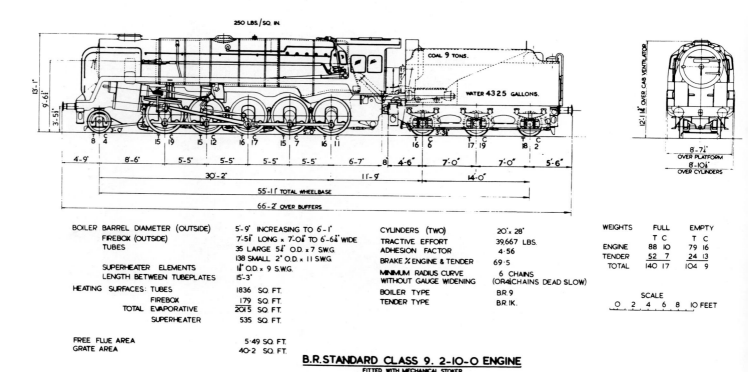

BOILER BARREL DIAMETER (OUTSIDE)	5'-9" INCREASING TO 6'-1"
FIREBOX (OUTSIDE)	7'-5½" LONG x 7'-0½" TO 6'-6¼" WIDE
TUBES	35 LARGE 5¼" O.D. x 7 S.W.G.
	138 SMALL 2" O.D x 11 S.W.G.
SUPERHEATER ELEMENTS	1⅛" O.D x 9 S.W.G.
LENGTH BETWEEN TUBEPLATES	15'-3"
HEATING SURFACES: TUBES	1836 SQ. FT.
FIREBOX	179 SQ. FT.
TOTAL EVAPORATIVE	2015 SQ. FT.
SUPERHEATER	535 SQ. FT.
FREE FLUE AREA	5·49 SQ. FT.
GRATE AREA	40·2 SQ. FT.

CYLINDERS (TWO)	20" x 28"
TRACTIVE EFFORT	39,667 LBS.
ADHESION FACTOR	4·56
BRAKE % ENGINE & TENDER	69·5
MINIMUM RADIUS CURVE WITHOUT GAUGE WIDENING	6 CHAINS (OR 4 CHAINS DEAD SLOW)
BOILER TYPE	BR.9
TENDER TYPE	B.R.1K.

WEIGHTS	FULL		EMPTY	
	T	C	T	C
ENGINE	88	10	79	16
TENDER	52	7	24	13
TOTAL	140	17	104	9

B.R. STANDARD CLASS 9. 2-10-0 ENGINE
FITTED WITH MECHANICAL STOKER

BR weight diagram SL/9R/6 for the three 9Fs fitted with the Berkley mechanical stoker, Nos.92165–67. This was the only 2–10–0 diagram showing the double chimney fitted to later engines.

Summary of Tests with BR Class 9F 2—10—0s at
Rugby Locomotive Testing Station

Loco No.	Run Nos.	Dates	Purpose of Test
92013	1118–1190	7/5/54 – 20/8/54	Performance & Efficiency
92015	1212–1228	12/10/54 – 27/10/54	Regulator modifications
92023	1352–1430	7/6/55 – 28/9/55	Crosti boiler
92050 (1)	1431–1468	7/10/55 – 15/11/55	Comparison with 92023
92050 (2)	1765–1803	6/3/57 – 26/4/57	Indicator reconciliation
92166	2063–2141	21/11/58 – 17/3/59	Berkley mechanical stoker
92250	2142–2257	9/4/59 – 1/9/59	Giesl oblong ejector*
92178	Swindon Plant	5/11/57 – 3/12/57	Double chimney

Giesl ejector fitted from run 2174, 21/5/59.

Brand–new Crosti No.92023 working all out on the Rugby plant, summer 1955. Note the specially installed large diameter chimney cowl, to accommodate the offset exhaust. R. Partridge Collection.

Appendix Three

BR Class 9F 2-10-0 Test Reports.

1. Basic Design (single exhaust):
(a) Performance & Efficiency Tests with Mobile Test Plant. Carlisle – Skipton Route, September 1954 CM and EE Dept. Derby Interim Report (L102) August 1955.
(b) Report on Tests of BR Standard Class 9 2-10-0 No.92015 with reduced Regulator Opening, Locomotive Testing Station, Rugby Report R9, November 1954.
(c) Trials with BR Std 2-10-0 Cl. 9F Locomotives hauling fitted 16 ton Mineral Wagons to Class C Timings, Toton – Brent. LMR No.3 Dynamometer Car, CM and EE Dept. Derby (L104) April 1955.
(d) Performance and Efficiency Tests with Exhaust Steam Injector, British Railways Standard Class 9F 2-Cylinder 2-10-0 Freight Locomotive, The British Standard Transport Commission, British Railways Bulletin No.13, July 1959.

2. Variants:
(a) Comparative Tests of British Railways Class 9 2-10-0 Locomotives No.92023 Fitted with a 'Crosti' Boiler and No.92050 Fitted with a BR Standard Boiler. May 1956.
(b) Tests to Determine Overall Fuel Consumption including Stand-By Losses BR Class 9F Crosti & Standard Locomotives. LMR Mobile Testing Plant CM and EE Dept. Derby (L108), undated.
(c) BR Standard Class 9 2-10-0 Locomotive fitted with Giesl Oblong Ejector, Comparative Tests, BR Locomotive Testing Station, Rugby, Report R 18, September 1959.
(d) BR Class 9 2-10-0 Locomotive fitted with Mechanical Stoker, British Railways Locomotive Testing Station, Rugby, Report R17, October 1959.

3. Other:
(a) Braking Tests with Loose Coupled Mineral trains, Toton – Brent, Type 4 2300 HP Diesel Electric and BR C1. 9F 2-10-0 Locomotives LMR No.1 Dynamometer Car, CM and EE Dept. Derby (L138) July 1960.

NB. No formal report was ever prepared concerning the provision of a double blastpipe and chimney on No.92178, although a file of the 'raw data' survives in the NRM Library.

Appendix Four

Dynamometer Car Tests with 9F 2-10-0s

A. LMR Dynamometer Car No. 3 (BR, 1949)
92013 Carlisle – Skipton – Carlisle with Mobile Test Unit, 28/9/54 – 22/10/54: Performance and Efficiency Tests.
92009 Toton – Brent – Toton 7/2/55 – 10/2/55: Loading Trials Class C Freights. [this engine suffered bent motion and was replaced by 92018]
92018 Toton – Brent – Toton 14/2/55 – 17/2/55: Loading Trials Class C Freights.
92023 Carlisle – Hurlford – Carlisle with Mobile Test Unit, 11/10/55 – 10/11/55: Evaluation of Crosti boiler.
92050 Carlisle – Hurlford – Carlisle with Mobile Test Unit, 22/11/55 – 9/12/55: Comparison with 92023.

B. WR Dynamometer Car (GW, 1901)
92002 Full Brake and Tender Handbrake Trials, 17/9/54.
92178 Reading – Stoke Gifford – Reading, Double Chimney, 28/1/58 – 7/2/58.
C. LMR Dynamometer Car No. 1 (LYR, 1913)
This vehicle was sometimes used in high speed freight trains hauled by various 9Fs, in pairs between Toton and Brent, c.1958.
92153 Toton – Brent Brake Tests 30/6/60.

D. ER Dynamometer Car (BR, 1951)
92196 Doncaster – New England – Doncaster 9-10/10/58. Locomotive load classification.
92200 Doncaster – New England – Doncaster 5-6/12/61. Timing trials.

Stoker–fired No. 92166 'at speed' in Rugby Test Plant, winter 1958/59. J.G. Click Collection, NRM.

No.92023 stands in steam outside the Rugby Test Plant during its summer 1955 tests. J. Mccann.

(*opposite*) Aesthetically, it could be argued, the original single chimney best suited the 9F, but the later double version undoubtedly enhanced performance. Unusually devoid of smoke deflectors, the first to be so fitted, No.92178, is recorded on a 14–coach test train (including the venerable GWR dynamometer car, at the end of its active career) on 31st January 1958. K.H. Leech.

The first double chimney 9F No.92178, on the stationary test plant at Swindon, 4th November 1957.

No.	Works. Order/Lot No.	To Traffic	1st Boiler	1st Tender	Cost	Allocations	Withdrawn	Cut–up
92000	CREWE E487	5/1/54	1128	1G/949	£23,975	Ebbw Jct. Bath Green Park 6/61. Banbury 9/61. Old Oak Common 3/62. Tyseley 7/62. Barrow Rd ?? Gloucester Horton Rd 2/65.	7/65	11/65
92001	— " —	12/1/54	1129	1G/950	– " –	Ebbw Jct. Bath Green Park 6/61. Canton 10/61. Bath Green Park 7/62. Oxford 10/62. Tyseley 11/62. Wakefield 10/66.	1/67	5/67
92002	— " —	16/1/54	1130	1G/951	– " –	Ebbw Jct. Tyseley 5/63. Banbury 7/64. Tyseley 11/64. Saltley 11/66. Birkenhead 12/66.	w.e. 11/11/67	4/68
92003	— " —	1/54	1131	1G/952	– " –	Ebbw Jct. Canton 11/58. Cardiff East Dock 9/62.	3/65	7/65
92004	— " —	30/1/54	1132	1G/953	– " –	Ebbw Jct. Canton 9/59. Southall 2/60. Ebbw Jct 10/60. Barrow Rd 1/61. Banbury 4/63. Kingmoor 10/66. Carnforth 1/68.	w.e. 23/3/68	7/68
92005	— " —	5/2/54	1133	1G/954	– " –	Ebbw Jct. Canton 11/58. Ebbw Jct 5/61. York 9/63.	30/8/65	12/65
92006	— " —	10/2/54	1134	1G/955	– " –	Ebbw Jct. Westbury 7/61. Ebbw Jct 9/61. York 9/63. Wakefield 10/66.	1/10/67	11/67
92007	— " —	2/54	1135	1G/956	– " –	Ebbw Jct. Barrow Rd 12/60. Gloucester Horton Rd 2/65. Cardiff East Dock 6/65. Severn Tunnel Jct 7/65. Gloucester Horton Rd 10/65.	12/65	2/66
92008	— " —	1/3/54	1136	1G/957	£23,882	Wellingborough. Saltley 6/57. Rowsley 11/59. Toton 2/62. Rowsley 3/62. Saltley 6/62. Rowsley 7/63. Kirkby-in-Ashfield 4/64. Speke Jct 12/64. Warrington 8/67.	w.e. 7/10/67	8/68
92009	— " —	12/3/54	1137	1G/958	– " –	Wellingborough. Saltley 6/57. Burton-on-Trent 9/57. Saltley 3/58. Annesley 10/58. Saltley 11/58. Rowsley 11/59. Saltley 6/62. Westhouses 7/62. Rowsley 10/63. Kettering 4/64. Kingmoor 5/64. Carnforth 1/68.	w.e. 23/3/68	7/68
92010	— " —	13/5/54	1138	1F/959	£23,828	March. Annesley 2/57. Wellingborough 3/63. Leicester Mid 6/63. Newton Heath 4/64. Kingmoor 6/64.	w.e. 2/4/66	6/66
92011	— " —	19/5/54	1139	1F/960	– " –	March. New England 9/55. Annesley 5/57. Birkenhead 8/65.	w.e. 11/11/67	1/68
92012	— " —	31/5/54	1140	1F/961	– " –	March. New England 9/55. Annesley 6/57. Rowsley 8/63. Kettering 4/64. Kingmoor 6/64.	w.e. 28/10/67	2/68
92013	— " —	23/4/54	1141	1F/962	– " –	On Test. March 11/54. Annesley 2/57. Woodford Halse 9/59. Annesley 10/59. Banbury 6/65. Saltley 9/66.	w.e. 1/10/66	5/67
92014	— " —	18/5/54	1142	1F/963	– " –	March. Stratford 7/54. March 1/56. Annesley 2/57. Saltley 3/60. Toton 9/60. Cricklewood 7/61. Annesley 10/61. Birkenhead 5/65.	w.e. 14/10/67	8/68
92015	CREWE E491	25/9/54	1143	1C/964	£23,655	Wellingborough. Saltley 11/57. Newton Heath 6/58. Bolton 9/62. Newton Heath 12/62. Kingmoor 6/64.	w.e. 29/4/67	11/67
92016	— " —	7/10/54	1144	1C/965	– " –	Wellingborough. Saltley 11/57. Newton Heath 6/58. Bolton 9/62. Newton Heath 12/62. Carnforth 6/67.	w.e. 21/10/67	4/68
92017	— " —	13/10/54	1145	1C/966	– " –	Wellingborough. Saltley 11/57. Newton Heath 6/58. Bolton 9/62. Newton Heath 12/62. Kingmoor 6/64.	w.e. 23/12/67	4/68
92018	— " —	21/10/54	1146	1C/967	– " –	Wellingborough. Cricklewood 11/57. Wellingborough 12/57. Rowsley 3/62. Kirkby-in-Ashfield 4/64. Newton Heath 9/64. Kingmoor 8/66.	w.e. 22/4/67	8/67
92019	— " —	25/10/54	1147	1C/968	– " –	Wellingborough. Cricklewood 11/57. Wellingborough 12/57. Toton 2/62. Wellingborough 3/62. Rowsley 3/62. Wellingborough 4/62. Kettering 1/64. Kingmoor 6/64.	w.e. 10/6/67	1/68
92020	CREWE E488	18/5/55	1148	1B/969	£25,584	Wellingborough. Kirkby-in-Ashfield 10/63. Speke Jct 9/64. Birkenhead 1/65.	w.e. 21/10/67	8/68
92021	— " —	18/5/55	1149	1B/970	– " –	Wellingborough. Kettering 1/64. Kingmoor 6/64. Birkenhead 7/65.	w.e. 11/11/67	1/68
92022	— " —	18/5/55	1150	1B/971	– " –	Wellingborough. Rowsley 7/63. Kettering 4/64. Newton Heath 6/64. Speke Jct 2/66. Birkenhead 2/67.	w.e. 11/11/67	4/68
92023	— " —	20/5/55	1151	1B/972	– " –	Wellingborough. On loan to Scottish Region during 12/55. Kettering 8/63. Kingmoor 5/64. Birkenhead 7/65.	w.e. 11/11/67	4/68
92024	— " —	6/6/55	1152	1B/973	– " –	Wellingborough. Kettering 1/64. Kingmoor 5/64. Birkenhead 7/65.	w.e. 11/11/67	5/68
92025	— " —	17/6/55	1153	1B/974	– " –	Wellingborough. Kettering 1/64. Annesley 4/64. Speke Jct 11/64. Birkenhead 2/67.	w.e. 11/11/67	4/68
92026	— " —	17/6/55	1154	1B/975	– " –	Wellingborough. Saltley 3/61. Wellingborough 5/61. Kettering 8/63. Kirkby-in-Ashfield 11/63. Newton Heath 9/64. Birkenhead 5/65.	w.e. 11/11/67	4/68
92027	— " —	25/6/55	1155	1B/976	– " –	Wellingborough. Kettering 1/64. Annesley 4/64. Speke Jct 11/64.	w.e. 5/8/67	12/67
92028	— " —	6/7/55	1156	1B/977	– " –	Wellingborough. Kettering 10/60. Saltley 10/62. Birkenhead 11/63. Saltley 4/64. Banbury 3/65. Saltley 7/65.	w.e. 22/10/66	1/67
92029	— " —	8/7/55	1157	1B/978	– " –	Wellingborough. Kettering 10/60. Saltley 10/62. Birkenhead 11/63. Saltley 4/64. Croes Newydd 6/66. Saltley 8/66. Birkenhead 12/66.	w.e. 11/11/67	2/68
92030	CREWE E489	3/11/54	1410	1F/1119	£23,266	New England. Annesley 6/57. Banbury 6/65. Tyseley 10/66. Wakefield 11/66.	2/67	7/67
92031	— " —	11/11/54	1411	1F/1120	– " –	March. New England 3/55. Annesley 5/57. Westhouses 6/65. Newton Heath 7/65.	w.e. 7/1/67	5/67
92032	— " —	17/11/54	1412	1F/1121	– " –	March. New England 12/54. Annesley 6/57. Kirkby-in-Ashfield 6/65. Birkenhead 7/65.	w.e. 15/4/67	10/67
92033	— " —	19/11/54	1413	1F/1122	– " –	March. New England 12/54. Annesley 6/57. Banbury 6/65. Northampton 7/65.	w.e. 18/9/65	12/65
92034	— " —	2/12/54	1414	1F/1123	– " –	New England. Frodingham 12/58. New England 4/59. Immingham 6/63.	w.e. 31/5/64	8/65
92035	— " —	3/12/54	1415	1F/1124	– " –	New England. Frodingham 12/58. New England 4/59. Immingham 6/63.	2/66	4/66
92036	— " —	3/12/54	1417	1F/1125	– " –	New England. Doncaster 9/62. Colwick 6/63. New England 10/63. Colwick 1/64. New England 6/64.	w.e. 6/12/64	5/65
92037	— " —	8/12/54	1418	1F/1126	– " –	New England. Immingham 6/63.	w.e. 21/2/65	6/65
92038	— " —	14/12/54	1419	1F/1127	– " –	New England. Immingham 6/63. New England 6/64. Langwith Jct 1/65.	w.e. 11/4/65	7/65
92039	— " —	17/12/54	1416	1F/1128	– " –	New England. Immingham 2/59. New England 8/61. Doncaster 9/62. Colwick 6/63. Immingham 11/63. Doncaster 6/64. Langwith Jct 1/65.	w.e. 17/10/65	1/66
92040	— " —	23/12/54	1421	1F/1129	– " –	New England. Colwick 6/63. Barrow Hill 9/64. Langwith Jct 1/65.	w.e. 8/8/65	11/65
92041	— " —	31/12/54	1422	1F/1130	– " –	New England. Colwick 6/63. Barrow Hill 9/64. Langwith Jct 1/65.	w.e. 29/8/65	11/65
92042	— " —	12/1/55	1423	1F/1131	– " –	New England. Colwick 6/63. Langwith Jct 1/65. Colwick 10/65.	12/65	4/66
92043	— " —	18/1/55	1424	1F/1132	– " –	March. Annesley 2/57. Burton-on-Trent 12/65. Kingmoor 1/66.	w.e. 30/7/66	10/66
92044	— " —	29/1/55	1425	1F/1133	– " –	March. New England 6/57. Doncaster 9/62. Colwick 6/63. Barrow Hill 1/65. Langwith Jct 1/65.	w.e. 11/4/65	7/65
92045	— " —	9/2/55	1426	1C/1134	– " –	Wellingborough. Toton 1/56. Bidston 5/56. Birkenhead 2/63.	w.e. 16/9/67	2/68
92046	— " —	11/2/55	1427	1C/1135	–"–	Wellingborough. Toton 1/56. Bidston 5/56. Birkenhead 2/63.	w.e. 21/10/67	8/68
92047	— " —	18/2/55	1428	1C/1136	– " –	Wellingborough. Bidston 8/55. Birkenhead 2/63.	w.e. 11/11/67	4/68
92048	— " —	26/2/55	1429	1C/1137	– " –	Wellingborough. Toton 1/56. Saltley 6/57. Rowsley 11/59. Toton 4/64. Warrington 3/65. Birkenhead 5/65.	w.e. 16/9/67	2/68
92049	— " —	10/3/55	1420	1C/1138	– " –	Wellingborough. Toton 1/56. Saltley 6/57. Rowsley 11/59. Toton 4/64. Warrington 3/65. Birkenhead 2/66.	w.e. 11/11/67	6/68
92050	CREWE E490	19/8/55	1430	1C/1139	£24,343	Toton. On loan to Scottish Region during 12/55. Rowsley 11/59. Kirkby-in-Ashfield 4/64. Newton Heath 10/64. Speke Jct 2/66. Warrington 8/67.	w.e. 30/9/67	2/68
92051	— " —	22/8/55	1431	1C/1140	– " –	Toton. Saltley 6/57. Rowsley 11/59. Kirkby-in-Ashfield 4/64. Newton Heath 10/64. Kingmoor 11/65.	w.e. 22/10/67	2/68
92052	— " —	26/8/55	1432	1C/1141	– " –	Toton. Wellingborough 3/58. Saltley 6/61. Annesley 10/61. Rowsley 4/62. Toton 4/62. Rowsley 7/63. Toton 7/63. Wellingborough 8/63. Kirkby-in-Ashfield 10/63. Newton Heath 10/64. Kingmoor 6/67.	w.e. 12/8/67	1/68

92053	— " —	17/9/55	1433 1C/1142	— " —	Toton. Burton-on-Trent 9/57. Saltley 3/58. Wellingborough 11/59. Toton 9/62. Warrington 3/65.	w.e. 19/2/66	12/66
92054	— " —	21/9/55	1434 1C/1143	— " —	Toton. Wellingborough 3/58. Westhouses 12/62. Kingmoor 5/64. Speke Jct 6/64.	w.e. 4/5/68	6/68
92055	— " —	22/9/55	1435 1C/1144	— " —	Toton. Wellingborough 3/58. Toton 9/60. Bidston 3/61. Toton 5/61. Rowsley 3/62. Toton 4/62. Wellingborough 7/62. Warrington 3/65. Speke Jct 10/67.	w.e. 23/12/67	4/68
92056	— " —	14/10/55	1436 1C/1145	— " —	Toton. Wellingborough 3/58. Toton 9/60. Saltley 4/62. Wellingborough 5/62. Rowsley 9/62. Kirkby-in-Ashfield 4/64. Newton Heath 10/64. Kingmoor 8/66.	w.e. 11/11/67	2/68
92057	— " —	11/10/55	1437 1C/1146	— " —	Toton. Westhouses 1/60. Cricklewood 5/60. Annesley 10/61. Toton 4/63. Saltley 10/63. Birkenhead 4/64.	w.e. 2/10/65	12/65
92058	— " —	13/10/55	1438 1C/1147	— " —	Toton. Wellingborough 3/58. Toton 9/60. Westhouses 7/62. Leicester Mid 4/64. Warrington 3/65. Speke Jct 6/67. Kingmoor 8/67.	w.e. 4/11/67	2/68
92059	— " —	20/10/55	1439 1C/1148	— " —	Toton. Wellingborough 3/58. Toton 9/60. Warrington 3/65. Birkenhead 5/65.	w.e. 17/9/66	1/67
92060	— " —	5/11/55	1440 1B/1149	£24,945	Tyne Dock. Wellingborough (on loan) 12/55. Tyne Dock 3/56.		10/66	4/67
92061	— " —	12/11/55	1441 1B/1150	— " —	Tyne Dock. Wellingborough (on loan) 12/55. Tyne Dock 3/56.	w.e. 4/9/66	11/66
92062	— " —	19/11/55	1442 1B/1151	— " —	Tyne Dock. Wellingborough (on loan) 12/55. Westhouses (on loan) 2/56. Tyne Dock 4/56.	w.e. 26/6/66	10/66
92063	— " —	25/11/55	1443 1B/1152	— " —	Tyne Dock. Wellingborough (on loan) 12/55. Westhouses (on loan) 2/56. Tyne Dock 5/56.	w.e. 24/11/66	4/67
92064	— " —	2/12/55	1444 1B/1153	— " —	Tyne Dock. Wellingborough (on loan) 12/55. Toton (on loan) 2/56. Tyne Dock 5/56.	w.e. 24/11/66	4/67
92065	— " —	10/12/55	1445 1B/1154	— " —	Tyne Dock. Wellingborough (on loan) 12/55. Toton (on loan) 2/56. Tyne Dock 5/56. Wakefield 11/66.	w.e. 3/4/67	8/67
92066	— " —	15/12/55	1446 1B/1155	— " —	Tyne Dock. Wellingborough (on loan) 12/55. Toton (on loan) 2/56. Tyne Dock 5/56.		5/65	9/65
92067	— " —	20/12/55	1447 1F/1156	£24,563	Doncaster. Annesley 2/57. Banbury 6/65. Kingmoor 10/66.	w.e. 5/11/66	2/67
92068	— " —	29/12/55	1448 1F/1157	— " —	Doncaster. Annesley 2/57. Kirkby-in-Ashfield 4/64. Annesley ?? Derby 12/65.	w.e. 15/1/66	4/66
92069	— " —	31/12/55	1449 1F/1158	— " —	Doncaster. Annesley 2/57. Birkenhead 5/65. Speke Jct 11/67.	w.e. 4/5/68	10/68
92070	— " —	14/1/56	1450 1F/1159	— " —	Doncaster. Annesley 2/57. Saltley 3/60. Toton 9/60. Westhouses 6/62. Wellingborough 3/63. Leicester Mid 5/63. Warrington 3/65. Birkenhead 5/65.	w.e. 11/11/67	2/68
92071	— " —	21/1/56	1451 1F/1160	— " —	Doncaster. Annesley 2/57. Newton Heath 7/65. Kingmoor 11/65.	w.e. 11/11/67	2/68
92072	— " —	1/2/56	1452 1F/1161	— " —	Doncaster. Annesley 2/57. Kirkby-in-Ashfield 6/65.	w.e. 8/1/66	6/66
92073	— " —	9/2/56	1453 1F/1162	— " —	Doncaster. Annesley 3/57. Banbury 6/65. Birkenhead 9/66.	w.e. 11/11/67	2/68
92074	— " —	18/2/56	1454 1F/1163	— " —	Doncaster. Annesley 3/57. Banbury 6/65. Saltley 12/65. Croes Newydd 6/66. Kingmoor 12/66.	w.e. 15/4/67	10/67
92075	— " —	1/3/56	1455 1F/1164	— " —	Doncaster. Annesley 3/57. Toton 4/63. Annesley 10/63. Kirkby-in-Ashfield 6/65. Kingmoor 4/66.	w.e. 17/9/66	2/67
92076	— " —	6/3/56	1456 1F/1165	— " —	Doncaster. Annesley 3/57. Rowsley 10/63. Kirkby-in-Ashfield 4/64. Newton Heath 10/64. Kingmoor 1/65.	w.e. 25/2/67	6/67
92077	— " —	13/3/56	1457 1F/1166	£24,343	Toton. Wellingborough 8/63. Kirkby-in-Ashfield 10/63. Newton Heath 6/64. Carnforth ??	w.e. 22/6/67	10/68
92078	— " —	21/3/56	1458 1F/1167	— " —	Toton. Warrington 3/65.	w.e. 6/5/67	1/68
92079	— " —	29/3/56	1459 1F/1168	— " —	Toton. Bromsgrove 5/56. Birkenhead 10/63.	w.e. 11/11/67	4/68
92080	— " —	14/4/56	1460 1C/1169	— " —	Toton. Wellingborough 3/58. Kettering 8/63. Newton Heath 6/64. Kingmoor 8/66.	w.e. 6/5/67	11/67
92081	— " —	23/4/56	1461 1C/1170	— " —	Toton. Annesley 11/58. Toton 5/59. Wellingborough 11/59. Kettering 8/63. Newton Heath 6/64.	w.e. 12/2/66	6/66
92082	— " —	3/5/56	1462 1C/1171	— " —	Wellingborough. Toton 2/62. Wellingborough 3/62. Saltley 2/63. Birkenhead 11/63.	w.e. 11/11/67	4/68
92083	— " —	11/5/56	1463 1C/1172	— " —	Wellingborough. Annesley 11/60. Wellingborough 3/61. Annesley 2/63. Wellingborough 3/63. Kettering 1/64. Leicester Mid 10/64. Annesley 1/65. Birkenhead 5/65.	w.e. 18/2/67	7/67
92084	— " —	19/5/56	1464 1C/1173	— " —	Wellingborough. Kettering 1/64. Speke Jct 9/64. Birkenhead 1/65.	w.e. 11/11/67	3/68
92085	— " —	26/5/56	1465 1C/1174	— " —	Wellingborough. Kettering 10/60. Saltley 10/62. Tyseley 11/63. Willesden 9/64. Birkenhead 12/64.	w.e. 24/12/66	7/80
92086	— " —	6/6/56	1466 1C/1175	— " —	Wellingborough. Kettering 1/64. Leicester Mid 10/64. Warrington 3/65. Birkenhead 6/65.	w.e. 11/11/67	4/68
92087	SWINDON 421*	29/8/56	1467 1F/1176	£29,699	Doncaster. Annesley 3/57. Banbury 6/65. Northampton 7/65. Tyseley 9/65. Carnforth 11/66.	w.e. 25/2/67	6/67
92088	— " —	24/10/56	1469 1F/1178	— " —	Doncaster. Annesley 3/57. Toton 5/63. Annesley 8/63. Toton 6/65. Birkenhead 7/65. Carnforth 11/67.	w.e. 27/4/68	10/68
92089	— " —	26/9/56	1468 1F/1177	— " —	Doncaster. Annesley 3/57. Leicester Mid 2/63. Speke Jct 9/64. Birkenhead 1/65.	w.e. 18/2/67	7/67
92090	— " —	8/11/56	1470 1F/1179	— " —	Doncaster. Annesley 3/57. Birkenhead 5/65.	w.e. 20/5/67	12/67
92091	— " —	27/11/56	1471 1F/1180	— " —	Doncaster. Annesley 3/57. Speke Jct 7/65. Carnforth 5/68.	w.e. 25/5/68	11/68
92092	— " —	13/12/56	1472 1F/1181	— " —	Doncaster. Annesley 3/57. Birkenhead 5/65.	w.e. 22/10/66	4/67
92093	— " —	15/1/57	1473 1F/1182	— " —	Doncaster. Annesley 3/57. Kirby-in-Ashfield 6/65. Kingmoor 1/66.	w.e. 2/9/67	2/68
92094	— " —	4/2/57	1474 1F/1183	— " —	Doncaster. Annesley 4/57. Toton 11/58. Annesley 5/59. Birkenhead 5/65. Speke Jct 11/67.	w.e. 4/5/68	9/68

A general view of Wellingborough shed yard on 29th April 1962, with five Class 9F 2–10–0s visible, including two converted Crostis. K.C.H. Fairey.

No.	Works. Order/Lot No.	To Traffic	1st Boiler	1st Tender	Cost	Allocations	Withdrawn	Cut-up
92095	— " —	6/3/57	1475	1F/1184	— " —	Annesley. Kirkby-in-Ashfield 6/65. Warrington 6/66.	w.e. 1/10/66	4/67
92096	— " —	2/4/57	1476	1F/1185	— " —	Annesley. Derby 12/65. Kingmoor 1/66.	w.e. 25/2/67	6/67
92097	CREWE E493	27/6/56	1644	1B/1307	£27,362	Tyne Dock.	w.e. 23/10/66	4/67
92098	— " —	4/7/56	1645	1B/1308	— " —	Tyne Dock.	w.e. 31/7/66	10/66
92099	— " —	23/7/56	1646	1B/1309	— " —	Tyne Dock.	w.e. 4/9/66	11/66
92100	— " —	30/7/56	1647	1C/1310	£26,344	Toton. Leicester Mid 3/58. Toton 12/59. Westhouses 1/60. Wellingborough 3/63. Leicester Mid 5/63. Birkenhead 4/65.	w.e. 13/5/67	1/68
92101	— " —	13/8/56	1648	1C/1311	— " —	Toton. Leicester Mid 3/58. Wellingborough 1/60. Leicester Mid 3/60. Birkenhead 4/65.	w.e. 14/10/67	8/68
92102	— " —	15/8/56	1649	1C/1312	— " —	Toton. Leicester Mid 3/58. Birkenhead 4/65.	w.e. 11/11/67	3/68
92103	— " —	18/8/56	1650	1C/1313	— " —	Toton. Leicester Mid 3/58. Birkenhead 4/65.	w.e. 27/5/67	6/68
92104	— " —	24/8/56	1651	1C/1314	— " —	Toton. Leicester Mid 3/58. Westhouses 4/62. Speke Jct 12/64. Birkenhead 4/65.	w.e. 25/2/67	7/67
92105	— " —	7/9/56	1652	1C/1315	— " —	Wellingborough. Kettering 11/56. Wellingborough 3/63. Kettering 1/64. Leicester Mid 10/64. Birkenhead 4/65.	w.e. 14/1/67	5/67
92106	— " —	12/9/56	1653	1C/1316	— " —	Wellingborough. Kettering 11/56. Leicester Mid 10/64. Birkenhead 4/65.	w.e. 29/7/67	12/67
92107	— " —	20/9/56	1654	1C/1317	— " —	Wellingborough. Saltley 12/61. Banbury 11/63. Willesden 9/64. Birkenhead 12/64.	w.e. 25/2/67	7/67
92108	— " —	12/10/56	1655	1C/1318	— " —	Wellingborough. Cricklewood 11/56. Wellingborough 5/59. Leicester Mid 3/60. Wellingborough 2/62. Birkenhead 4/65.	w.e. 11/11/67	2/68
92109	— " —	15/10/56	1656	1C/1319	— " —	Toton. Saltley 3/57. Wellingborough 6/57. Leicester Mid 8/59. Annesley 11/63. Leicester Mid 4/64. Birkenhead 4/65.	w.e. 11/11/67	3/68
92110	— " —	23/10/56	1657	1C/1320	— " —	Toton. Cricklewood 11/56. Wellingborough 5/59. Leicester Mid 3/60. Wellingborough 7/62. Annesley 11/63. Newton Heath 9/64. Kingmoor 5/65.	w.e. 30/12/67	3/68
92111	— " —	6/11/56	1658	1C/1321	— " —	Cricklewood. Wellingborough 5/59. Leicester Mid 3/60. Annesley 11/63. Speke Jct 9/64. Birkenhead 1/65.	w.e. 28/10/67	2/68
92112	— " —	17/11/56	1659	1C/1322	— " —	Cricklewood. Wellingborough 5/59. Leicester Mid 3/60. Birkenhead 4/65.	w.e. 11/11/67	3/68
92113	— " —	24/11/56	1660	1C/1323	— " —	Westhouses. Toton 6/60. Bidston 3/61. Toton 5/61. Rowsley 4/62. Toton 2/64. Annesley 10/64. Westhouses (store) 6/65. Birkenhead 7/65.	w.e. 7/10/67	8/68
92114	— " —	29/11/56	1661	1C/1324	— " —	Westhouses. Toton 6/60. Rowsley 4/62. Kirkby-in-Ashfield 4/64. Newton Heath 9/64. Kingmoor 5/65.	w.e. 22/7/67	2/68
92115	— " —	12/12/56	1662	1C/1325	— " —	Westhouses. Kingmoor 5/64. Speke Jct 6/64.	w.e. 19/2/66	6/66
92116	— " —	22/12/56	1663	1C/1326	— " —	Westhouses. Wellingborough 3/63. Kettering 2/64. Warrington 3/65.	w.e. 12/11/66	7/67
92117	— " —	27/12/56	1664	1C/1327	— " —	Westhouses. Annesley 10/61. Rowsley 3/62. Wellingborough 4/62. Toton 2/64. Speke Jct 10/64.	w.e. 23/12/67	4/68
92118	— " —	28/12/56	1665	1C/1328	— " —	Westhouses. Wellingborough 11/59. Saltley 1/62. Banbury 7/64. Tyseley 11/64. Carnforth 11/66.	w.e. 25/5/68	9/68
92119	— " —	12/1/57	1666	1C/1329	— " —	Westhouses. Cricklewood 1/59. Leicester Mid 4/59. Warrington 3/65. Speke Jct 6/67. Kingmoor 8/67.	w.e. 23/9/67	2/68
92120	— " —	28/1/57	1667	1C/1330	— " —	Westhouses. Annesley 10/58. Westhouses 11/58. Saltley 11/58. Wellingborough 11/59. Leicester Mid 6/60. Annesley 11/60. Leicester Mid 10/61. Birkenhead 4/65.	w.e. 8/7/67	2/68
92121	— " —	8/2/57	1668	1C/1331	— " —	Wellingborough. Saltley 3/57. Wellingborough 6/57. Leicester Mid 8/57. Birkenhead 4/65.	w.e. 29/7/67	1/68
92122	— " —	18/2/57	1669	1C/1332	— " —	Wellingborough. Leicester Mid 3/60. Wellingborough 7/62. Birkenhead 4/65.	w.e. 11/11/67	2/68
92123	— " —	26/2/57	1670	1C/1333	— " —	Wellingborough. Leicester Mid 3/60. Birkenhead 4/65.	w.e. 28/10/67	2/68
92124	— " —	2/3/57	1671	1C/1334	— " —	Wellingborough. Kettering 2/64. Warrington 3/65.	w.e. 3/12/66	4/67
92125	— " —	9/3/57	1672	1C/1335	— " —	Wellingborough. Kettering 10/60. Saltley 11/63. Croes Newydd 6/66. Kingmoor 12/66.	w.e. 30/12/67	4/68
92126	— " —	18/3/57	1673	1C/1336	— " —	Wellingborough. Toton 2/64. Warrington 3/65.	w.e. 5/8/67	1/68
92127	— " —	29/3/57	1674	1C/1337	— " —	Wellingborough. Rowsley 7/63. Kirkby-in-Ashfield 4/64. Speke Jct 10/64. Birkenhead 1/65.	w.e. 19/8/67	12/67
92128	— " —	5/4/57	1675	1C/1338	— " —	Toton. Leicester Mid 3/58. Saltley 6/62. Banbury 7/64. Saltley 9/66. Carnforth 11/66.	w.e. 11/11/67	5/68
92129	— " —	10/4/57	1676	1C/1339	— " —	Saltley. Toton 6/57. Kettering 7/59. Toton 2/60. Cricklewood 5/60. Annesley 10/61. Saltley 12/61. Banbury 7/64. Kingmoor 9/66.	w.e. 1/7/67	11/67
92130	— " —	15/4/57	1677	1C/1340	— " —	Saltley. Toton 6/57. Kingmoor 5/64.	w.e. 14/6/66	11/66
92131	— " —	25/4/57	1678	1C/1341	— " —	Saltley. Toton 6/57. Westhouses 1/60. Speke Jct 12/64. Birkenhead 5/65.	w.e. 23/9/67	2/68
92132	— " —	29/4/57	1679	1C/1342	— " —	Saltley. Wellingborough 11/57. Kettering 2/64. Annesley 3/64. Banbury 6/65. Northampton 8/65. Banbury 9/65. Warrington 8/66. Kingmoor 10/67.	w.e. 21/10/67	2/68
92133	— " —	22/5/57	1680	1C/1343	— " —	Saltley. Wellingborough 11/57. Leicester Mid 2/64. Birkenhead 4/65.	w.e. 22/7/67	1/68
92134	— " —	24/5/57	1681	1C/1344	— " —	Saltley. Wellingborough 11/57. Leicester Mid 2/64. Birkenhead 4/65.	w.e. 10/12/66	—
92135	CREWE E494	11/6/57	1682	1C/1345	£27,871	Saltley. Croes Newydd 6/66. Wakefield 10/66.	6/67	3/68
92136	— " —	18/6/57	1683	1C/1346	— " —	Saltley.	w.e. 29/10/66	2/67
92137	— " —	24/6/57	1684	1C/1347	— " —	Saltley. Croes Newydd 8/66. Kingmoor 12/66.	w.e. 9/9/67	2/68
92138	— " —	25/6/57	1685	1C/1348	— " —	Saltley. Speke Jct 8/66.	w.e. 8/7/67	2/68
92139	— " —	28/6/57	1686	1C/1349	— " —	Saltley. Speke Jct 12/66. Kingmoor 8/67.	w.e. 9/9/67	2/68
92140	— " —	5/7/57	1687	1F/1350	— " —	New England. Langwith Jct 1/65.	w.e. 11/4/65	7/65
92141	— " —	29/7/57	1688	1F/1351	— " —	New England. Doncaster 9/62. New England 3/63. Langwith Jct 1/65. Colwick 10/65.	12/65	4/66

Number	Builder	Date	Works No.	Price	Allocation	Withdrawn	Disposal
92142	— " —	29/7/57	1689 1F/1352	— " —	New England.	w.e. 21/2/65	2/66
92143	— " —	10/8/57	1690 1F/1353	— " —	New England.	w.e. 21/2/65	5/65
92144	— " —	19/8/57	1691 1F/1354	— " —	New England. Immingham 9/62. New England 3/63. Langwith Jct 1/65. Colwick 10/65.	12/65	4/66
92145	— " —	26/8/57	1692 1F/1355	— " —	New England. Langwith Jct 1/65. Colwick 10/65. Immingham 12/65.	2/66	4/66
92146	— " —	5/9/57	1693 1F/1356	— " —	New England. Langwith Jct 1/65. Colwick 10/65. Doncaster 12/65.	w.e. 17/4/66	8/66
92147	— " —	14/9/57	1695 1F/1357	— " —	New England. Immingham 3/63.	w.e. 4/4/65	8/65
92148	— " —	21/9/57	1694 1F/1358	— " —	New England. Immingham 6/60. New England 8/61. Doncaster 3/63. Colwick 6/63. Barrow Hill 9/64. Langwith Jct 1/65. Colwick 10/65.	12/65	4/66
92149	— " —	1/10/57	1696 1F/1359	— " —	New England. Langwith Jct 1/65.	w.e. 27/6/65	10/65
92150	— " —	5/10/57	1697 1C/1271	— " —	Westhouses. Saltley 1/59. Tyseley 5/64. Saltley 6/64. Wakefield 10/66.	4/67	11/67
92151	— " —	9/10/57	1698 1C/1361	— " —	Saltley. Birkenhead 11/66.	w.e. 22/4/67	4/68
92152	— " —	16/10/57	1699 1C/1362	— " —	Saltley. Birkenhead 11/66.	w.e. 11/11/67	3/68
92153	— " —	21/10/57	1700 1C/1363	— " —	Toton. Westhouses 10/63. Speke Jct 6/65.	w.e. 20/1/68	6/68
92154	— " —	28/10/57	1701 1C/1364	— " —	Wellingborough. Annesley 5/58. Wellingborough 9/58. Annesley 2/64. Speke Jct 7/65.	w.e. 22/7/67	1/68
92155	— " —	5/11/57	1702 1C/1365	— " —	Saltley. Kirkby-in-Ashfield 6/65. Speke Jct 8/66.	w.e. 19/11/66	4/67
92156	— " —	15/11/57	1703 1C/1366	— " —	Toton. Warrington 3/65.	w.e. 22/7/67	3/68
92157	— " —	20/11/57	1704 1C/1367	— " —	Toton. Saltley 1/59. Birkenhead 4/64.	w.e. 19/8/67	1/68
92158	— " —	22/11/57	1705 1C/1368	— " —	Toton. Westhouses 9/63. Speke Jct 5/64.	w.e. 23/7/66	11/66
92159	— " —	27/11/57	1706 1C/1369	— " —	Wellingborough. Cricklewood 11/58. Wellingborough 12/58. Rowsley 2/64. Kirkby-in-Ashfield 4/64. Newton Heath 9/64. Birkenhead 11/66.	w.e. 22/7/67	1/68
92160	— " —	29/11/57	1707 1C/1370	— " —	Wellingborough. Kettering 9/58. Warrington 3/65. Birkenhead 2/66. Carnforth 11/67. Speke Jct 11/67. Carnforth 5/68.	w.e. 29/6/68	10/68
92161	— " —	17/12/57	1708 1C/1371	— " —	Westhouses. Newton Heath 6/58. Kingmoor 5/65.	w.e. 10/12/66	5/67
92162	— " —	19/12/57	1709 1C/1360	— " —	Westhouses. Newton Heath 6/58. Kingmoor 5/65.	w.e. 11/11/67	5/68
92163	— " —	24/3/58	1710 1C/1372	— " —	Kettering. Leicester Mid 6/59. Kettering 11/59. Warrington 3/65. Birkenhead 6/65.	w.e. 30/7/66	10/66
92164	— " —	1/4/58	1711 1C/1373	— " —	Leicester Mid. Saltley 6/62.	w.e. 16/3/68	6/68
92165	— " —	17/4/58	1712 1K/1375	£30,308	Saltley. Bidston 6/62. Birkenhead 2/63. Speke Jct 11/67.		
92166	— " —	24/5/58	1714 1K/1376	— " —	Saltley. Rugby Test Plant 8/58. Saltley 6/59. Ebbw Jct (on loan) 9/59. Saltley 2/60. Bidston 6/62. Birkenhead 2/63.	w.e. 11/11/67	3/68
92167	— " —	9/5/58	1713 1K/1377	— " —	Saltley. Tyne Dock (on loan) 5/62. Saltley 10/62. Bidston 12/62. Birkenhead 2/63. Carnforth 11/67.	w.e. 29/6/68	11/68
92168	— " —	20/12/57	1715†1F/1374	£27,871	Doncaster.	w.e. 27/6/65	11/65
92169	— " —	27/12/57	1716 1F/1378	— " —	Doncaster.	w.e. 31/5/64	1/65
92170	— " —	31/12/57	1718 1F/1379	— " —	Doncaster.	w.e. 31/5/64	1/65
92171	— " —	1/2/58	1717 1F/1380	— " —	Doncaster. New England 11/63.	w.e. 31/5/64	3/65
92172	— " —	29/1/58	1719 1F/1381	— " —	Doncaster.	w.e. 17/4/66	7/66
92173	— " —	10/2/58	1720 1F/1382	— " —	Doncaster. Langwith Jct 6/65. Colwick 10/65. Doncaster 12/65.	w.e. 6/3/66	5/66
92174	— " —	10/2/58	1721 1F/1383	— " —	Doncaster.	w.e. 12/12/65	5/66
92175	— " —	21/2/58	1723 1F/1384	— " —	Doncaster.	w.e. 31/5/64	2/65
92176	— " —	4/3/58	1722 1F/1385	— " —	Doncaster. New England 11/63.	w.e. 31/5/64	3/65
92177	— " —	12/3/58	1724 1F/1386	— " —	Doncaster.	w.e. 31/5/64	8/64
92178	SWINDON 422	28/9/57	1725 1F/1388	£32,845	New England. Langwith Jct 1/65.	10/65	12/65
92179	— " —	7/10/57	1726 1F/1389	— " —	New England. Langwith Jct 1/65. Colwick 10/65.	11/65	5/66
92180	— " —	8/11/57	1727 1F/1390	— " —	New England. Langwith Jct 1/65.	w.e. 11/4/65	7/65
92181	— " —	22/11/57	1728 1F/1391	— " —	New England.	w.e. 21/2/65	7/65
92182	— " —	3/12/57	1729 1F/1392	— " —	New England. Langwith Jct 1/65. Colwick 10/65. Doncaster 12/65.	w.e. 17/4/66	7/66
92183	— " —	20/12/57	1730 1F/1393	— " —	New England. Colwick 6/63. Doncaster 1/65.	w.e. 3/4/66	7/66
92184	— " —	10/1/58	1731 1F/1394	— " —	New England. Frodingham 12/58. New England 6/59. Colwick 6/63. New England 10/63. Immingham 1/64.	2/65	6/65
92185	— " —	15/1/58	1732 1F/1395	— " —	New England. Colwick 6/63. New England 10/63. Immingham 1/64.	w.e. 21/2/65	6/65
92186	— " —	27/1/58	1733 1F/1396	— " —	New England. Colwick 6/63. Doncaster 1/65. Langwith Jct 6/65.	w.e. 29/8/65	2/66
92187	— " —	12/2/58	1734 1F/1397	— " —	New England. Grantham 6/58. New England 8/58. Colwick 6/63.	w.e. 21/2/65	5/65
92188	— " —	27/2/58	1735 1F/1398	— " —	New England. Grantham 6/58. New England 8/58. Colwick 6/63.	w.e. 21/2/65	5/65
92189	— " —	14/3/58	1736 1F/1399	— " —	Mexborough. Darnall 4/58. Doncaster 5/58. Frodingham 12/58. Doncaster 4/59. Colwick 9/63. Langwith Jct 1/65. Colwick 10/65.	12/65	4/66
92190	— " —	28/3/58	1737 1F/1400	— " —	Mexborough. Darnall 4/58. Doncaster 5/58. Frodingham 12/58. Doncaster 5/59. Colwick 9/63. Doncaster 6/64.	w.e. 10/10/65	1/66
92191	— " —	15/4/58	1738 1F/1401	— " —	Darnall. Doncaster 5/58. Colwick 9/63. Langwith Jct 1/65. Colwick 10/65.	12/65	4/66
92192	— " —	1/5/58	1739 1F/1402	— " —	Doncaster. Colwick 9/63. Frodingham 11/63.	w.e. 21/2/65	5/65
92193	— " —	23/5/58	1740 1F/1403	— " —	Doncaster. Immingham 2/59.	w.e. 13/6/65	11/65
92194	— " —	10/6/58	1741 1F/1404	— " —	Doncaster. Immingham 2/59. New England 6/64. Langwith Jct 1/65.	w.e. 5/12/65	3/66
92195	— " —	27/6/58	1742 1F/1405	— " —	Doncaster. Immingham 2/59.	w.e. 9/5/65	11/65
92196	— " —	15/8/58	1743 1F/1406	— " —	Doncaster. Frodingham 2/59. Doncaster 5/59. Immingham 9/60.	w.e. 6/12/64	1/66
92197	— " —	11/9/58	1744 1F/1407	— " —	Doncaster. Frodingham 2/59. Doncaster 5/59. Colwick 9/63. Frodingham 11/63.	w.e. 19/9/65	1/66
92198	— " —	6/10/58	1877 1F/1408	— " —	Doncaster. Colwick 9/63. Frodingham 11/63.	w.e. 2/8/64	6/65
92199	— " —	29/10/58	1745 1F/1409	— " —	Doncaster. Immingham 9/63. Doncaster 6/64. Langwith Jct 6/65.	w.e. 2/8/64	6/65
92200	— " —	18/11/58	1746 1F/1410	— " —	Doncaster. Immingham 9/63. Doncaster 6/64.	w.e. 3/10/65	12/65
92201	— " —	5/12/58	1747 1F/1411	— " —	Doncaster. Immingham 3/59.	w.e. 27/3/66	7/66
92202	— " —	27/12/58	1748 1F/1412	— " —	Doncaster. Immingham 3/59.	w.e. 19/12/65	3/66
92203	SWINDON 429	6/4/59	1749 1G/1510	£33,497	St Philips Marsh. Old Oak Common 9/60. Banbury 4/63. Birkenhead 9/66.	w.e. 11/11/67	—
92204	— " —	21/4/59	1879 1G/1511	— " —	St Philips Marsh. Southall 9/60. Old Oak Common 10/60. Banbury 9/63. Tyseley 9/63. Speke Jct 8/66.	w.e. 9/12/67	3/68
92205	— " —	4/59	1880 1G/1512	— " —	St Philips Marsh. Westbury 9/60. Eastleigh 12/60. Feltham 6/63. York 9/63. Wakefield 10/66.	w.e. 8/6/67	2/68
92206	— " —	5/59	1881 1G/1513	— " —	St Philips Marsh. Westbury 9/60. Eastleigh 12/60. Feltham 6/63. York 9/63. Wakefield 10/66.	w.e. 9/5/67	9/67
92207	— " —	5/59	1882 1G/1514	— " —	St Philips Marsh. Southall 2/60. Ebbw Jct 11/64.	12/64	—
92208	— " —	11/6/59	1883 1G/1515	— " —	Laira. Southall 3/60. Canton 11/61. Cardiff East Dock 9/62. Newton Heath 10/63. Kingmoor 6/64.	w.e. 28/11/67	2/68
92209	— " —	6/59	1884 1G/1516	— " —	Laira. Canton 8/59. Ebbw Jct 5/61. Cardiff East Dock 9/63. Southall 5/65. Cardiff East Dock 6/65. Severn Tunnel Jct 7/65. Barrow Road 10/65.	12/65	3/66
92210	— " —	8/59	1885 1G/1517	— " —	Canton. Barrow Road 9/60. Bath Green Park 7/62. Canton 8/62. Cardiff East Dock 9/62. Southall 12/65. Ebbw Jct 5/64.	11/64	3/65
92211	— " —	9/59	1886 1G/1518	— " —	Old Oak Common. Westbury 9/61. Feltham 6/63. York 9/63. Wakefield 10/66.	w.e. 22/5/67	12/67
92212	— " —	22/9/59	1887 1G/1519	— " —	Banbury. Bath Green Park 6/61. Ebbw Jct 9/61. Tyseley 7/62. Carnforth 11/66.	w.e. 6/1/68	—
92213	— " —	22/10/59	1888 1G/1520	— " —	Banbury. Kingmoor 10/66.	w.e. 5/11/66	2/67
92214	— " —	10/59	1889 1G/1521	— " —	Banbury. Ebbw Jct 11/61. Severn Tunnel Jct 7/64.	w.e. 9/8/65	—

No.	Works. Order/Lot No.	To Traffic	1st Boiler	1st Tender	Cost	Allocations	Withdrawn	Cut-up
92215	— " —	17/11/59	1890	1G/1522	– " –	Banbury. Tyseley 9/63. Wakefield 10/66.	6/67	3/68
92216	— " —	12/59	1891	1G/1523	– " –	Canton. Cardiff East Dock 9/62. Neath Court Sart 10/63. Southall 9/64. Severn Tunnel Jct 8/65.	10/65	4/66
92217	— " —	22/12/59	1892	1G/1524	– " –	Canton. St Philips Marsh 1/60. Banbury 4/63. Tyseley 9/63.	w.e. 30/7/66	10/66
92218	— " —	1/60	1893	1G/1525	– " –	St Philips Marsh. Banbury 4/63. Warrington 10/66. Speke Jct 3/67. Kingmoor 8/67. Speke Jct 1/68.	5/68	7/68
92219	— " —	1/60	1894	1G/1526	– " –	St Philips Marsh. Canton 2/60. Cardiff East Dock 9/62.	8/65	—
92220	— " —	25/3/60	1895	1G/1527	– " –	Canton. Bath Green Park 8/62. Old Oak Common 10/62. Oxford 11/62. Bath Green Park 8/63. Cardiff East Dock 10/63.	w.e. 29/3/65	—
92221	CREWE E497	5/58	1912	1G/1532	£30,200	Banbury. Laira 7/59. Banbury 3/60. Laira 6/60. Westbury 9/60. Banbury 10/60. Barrow Rd 11/60. York 9/63.	5/65	9/65
92222	— " —	6/58	1913	1G/1533	– " –	Banbury. Laira 7/59. Banbury 3/60. Laira 6/60. Ebbw Jct 10/60. Neath Court Sart 11/63. Southall 9/64.	3/65	7/65
92223	— " —	6/6/58	1914	1G/1534	– " –	Banbury. Laira 7/59. Banbury 3/60. Laira 6/60. Westbury 9/60. Ebbw Jct 3/61. Bromsgrove 10/63. Tyseley 5/64. Saltley 11/66. Kingmoor 12/66. Carnforth 1/68.	w.e. 13/4/68	9/68
92224	— " —	6/58	1915	1G/1535	– " –	Banbury. Laira 7/59. Southall 7/60. Oxford 10/62. Bath Green Park 8/63. Barrow Rd 9/63. Cardiff East Dock 10/63. Banbury 11/64. Warrington 8/66.	w.e. 30/9/67	6/68
92225	— " —	6/58	1916	1G/1536	– " –	Banbury. Laira 7/59. Ebbw Jct 3/60. Neath Court Sart 10/63. Ebbw Jct 5/64.	7/65	9/65
92226	— " —	6/58	1917	1G/1537	– " –	Banbury. Southall 7/60. Ebbw Jct 10/60. Old Oak Common 10/61. Ebbw Jct 11/62. Southall 11/63. Ebbw Jct 5/64. Severn Tunnel Jct 7/64. Ebbw Jct 10/64. Severn Tunnel Jct 6/65.	9/65	2/66
92227	— " —	3/7/58	1919	1G/1538	– " –	Banbury. Canton 1/61. Banbury 8/62. Warrington 10/66. Speke Jct 3/67.	w.e. 4/11/67	1/68
92228	— " —	12/7/58	1918	1G/1539	– " –	Banbury. Speke Jct 10/66.	w.e. 28/2/67	6/67
92229	— " —	7/58	1920	1G/1540	– " –	Banbury. Old Oak Common 11/58. Ebbw Jct 1/60. Southall 11/63. Ebbw Jct 5/64.	11/64	2/65
92230	— " —	8/58	1921	1G/1541	– " –	Banbury. Old Oak Common 11/58. Old Oak Common 10/62. Ebbw Jct 11/62. Bromsgrove 1/64. Ebbw Jct 8/64. Gloucester Horton Rd 10/65.	12/65	7/66
92231	— " —	1/8/58	1922	1G/1542	– " –	Pontypool Rd. Severn Tunnel Jct 1/59. Canton 2/59. Ebbw Jct 10/59. Canton 2/60. Barrow Rd 10/60. Eastleigh 12/60. Feltham 6/63. York 9/63.	w.e. 17/11/66	4/67
92232	— " —	8/58	1923	1G/1543	– " –	Pontypool Rd. Severn Tunnel Jct 1/59. Canton 2/59. Banbury 9/59. Cardiff East Dock 9/62.	12/64	3/65
92233	— " —	11/8/58	1924	1G/1544	– " –	Pontypool Rd. Severn Tunnel Jct 1/59. Canton 2/59. Banbury 9/59. Canton 1/61. Bath Green Park 7/62. Ebbw Jct 10/62. Newton Heath 10/63. Kingmoor 6/64. Speke Jct 1/68.	w.e. 3/2/68	8/68
92234	— " —	19/8/58	1925	1G/1545	– " –	Pontypool Rd. Severn Tunnel Jct 1/59. Canton 2/59. Banbury 9/59. Bromsgrove 9/61. Banbury 11/61. Tyseley 8/62. Banbury 9/64. Tyseley 9/66. Birkenhead 12/66.	w.e. 11/11/67	2/68
92235	— " —	8/58	1926	1G/1546	– " –	Pontypool Rd. Severn Tunnel Jct 1/59. Canton 2/59. Ebbw Jct 9/59. Barrow Rd 10/65.	11/65	4/66
92236	— " —	9/58	1927	1G/1547	– " –	Pontypool Rd. Ebbw Jct 10/58. Canton 11/58. Cardiff East Dock 9/62. Severn Tunnel Jct 11/64.	4/65	10/65
92237	— " —	9/58	1928	1G/1548	– " –	Ebbw Jct. Canton 11/58. Cardiff East Dock 9/62. Severn Tunnel Jct 11/64. Ebbw Jct 2/65.	9/65	11/65
92238	— " —	9/58	1929	1G/1549	– " –	Ebbw Jct. Old Oak Common 12/58. Southall 9/60. Ebbw Jct 12/61. Barrow Road 10/63. Severn Tunnel Jct 7/65.	9/65	12/65
92239	— " —	25/9/58	1930	1G/1550	– " –	Ebbw Jct. Old Oak Common 12/58. Southall 9/60. Westbury 7/61. Feltham 6/63. York 9/63.	11/66	4/67
92240	— " —	1/10/58	1931	1G/1551	– " –	Ebbw Jct. Old Oak Common 12/58. Southall 9/60.	8/65	—
92241	— " —	10/58	1932	1G/1552	– " –	Ebbw Jct. Old Oak Common 12/58. Canton 9/60. Cardiff East Dock 9/62. Southall 11/63.	7/65	12/65
92242	— " —	10/58	1933	1G/1553	– " –	Ebbw Jct. Severn Tunnel Jct 10/64.	5/65	8/65
92243	— " —	10/58	1934	1G/1554	– " –	Ebbw Jct. Old Oak Common 11/62. Cardiff East Dock 9/63. Severn Tunnel Jct 11/64. Cardiff East Dock 1/65. Severn Tunnel Jct 7/65. Barrow Road 10/65.	12/65	4/66
92244	— " —	10/58	1935	1G/1555	– " –	Ebbw Jct. Old Oak Common 12/58. Canton 10/60. Cardiff East Dock 9/62. Oxford 10/62. Cardiff East Dock 11/62. Severn Tunnel Jct 7/65. Gloucester Horton Rd 10/65.	12/65	7/66
92245	— " —	11/58	1936	1G/1556	– " –	Old Oak Common. Canton 10/60. Bath Green Park 5/62. Oxford 10/62. Southall 11/62.	12/65	—
92246	— " —	11/58	1937	1G/1557	– " –	Old Oak Common. Canton 10/60. Cardiff East Dock 9/62. Southall 11/63. Severn Tunnel Jct 8/65. Gloucester Horton Rd 10/65.	12/64	4/66
92247	— " —	2/12/58	1938	1G/1558	– " –	Old Oak Common. Canton 2/62. Banbury 8/62. Newton Heath 9/66.	12/65	4/67
92248	— " —	12/58	1939	1G/1559	– " –	Ebbw Jct. Saltley 9/59 (on loan). Ebbw Jct 11/59. Barrow Road 9/60. Cardiff East Dock 1/65.	w.e. 8/10/66	8/65
92249	— " —	10/12/58	1940	1G/1560	– " –	Ebbw Jct. Laira 6/60. Ebbw Jcy 10/60. Newton Heath 10/63. Kingmoor 6/64. Speke Jct 1/68.	5/65	9/68
92250	— " —	16/12/58	1941	1G/1561	– " –	Banbury. Rugby Testing Stn 5/59. Ebbw Jct 11/59. Southall 11/63. Ebbw Jct 5/64. Severn Tunnel Jct 7/64. Gloucester Horton Rd 10/65.	w.e. 4/5/68	12/65
							12/65	7/66

Notes:-

* Order transferred from Crewe February 1954.

† This tender ran as 1F/1377 from 20/12/57 to 2/6/58.

(NER) No.92065 and an unidentified companion rest at Tyne Dock in September 1963.

Appendix Six

Annual Returns of BR Class 9F 2–10–0
Book Stock by Region, 1954 – 1967

Year Dec 31	LMR	ER	WR	NER	SR	Total	Change
1954	7	17	8	—	—	32	32
1955	22	23	8	7	—	70	+38
1956	61	46	8	10	—	115	+45
1957	95	55	8	10	—	171	+56
1958*	129	55	39	10	—	233	+62
1959	129	55	54	10	—	248	+15
1960	129	55	57	10	—	251	+3
1961	129	55	54	10	3	251	0
1962	129	55	52	10	5	251	0
1963	147	55	31	18	—	251	0
1964	147	44	26	18	—	235	−16
1965	136	19	0	15	—	170	−75
1966	105	0	—	10	—	125	−45
1967	18	—	—	0	—	18	−107
(1)	100	85	56	10	0	251	
(2)	144	55	29	23	0	251	

(1) = Total authorised for. (2) = Total withdrawn.
* Owing to regional boundary changes in 1958 the LMR gained the 30 9Fs at Annesley (formerly ER) and lost one 9F (92079) at Bromsgrove which became WR stock. The year 1958 also witnessed the peak of 9F construction by which time it was the only class of steam locomotive still being built by BR.

Appendix Seven

British Railways Traction Costs

Year	1950	1954	1958	1962
STEAM				
Total traction miles	335·3m	328·5m	289·6m	180·2m
Coal consumption (tons)	13,748,000	12,915,000	10,745,000	6,273,000
Fuel costs	£35,908,103	£46,195,372	£62,805,367	£44,264,925
Crew wages	£41,075,262	£50,460,477	£39,625,248	£29,333,437
Totals	£76,983,365	£96,655,849	£102,430,615	£73,598,362
Cost per traction mile	23·0p	29·4p	35·4p	40·9p
DIESEL (inc DMU)				
Total traction miles			32·5m	148·4m
Fuel costs			£1,413,786	£5,604,088
Crew wages			£3,142,325	£14,684,451
Totals			£4,556,111	£20,288,539
Cost per traction mile			14·0p	13·7p

The Annual Report & Accounts of the British Transport Commission for the period 1948 to 1956 gave a fairly detailed breakdown of the cost of steam locomotive operation on BR during its early years. After 1956 fuel costs overtook wages as the dominant factor, peaking at £63·8 million in 1957 when steam traction miles were 10% down on the 1948 figure. By this time, weighted by diesel railcar operation, diesel traction operating costs amounted to roughly only 40% of those for steam, despite the considerably greater (roughly three–fold) capital cost of equivalent new diesel *locomotives*.

Given below is a breakdown of the operating costs in 1955 of the British railways steam locomotive fleet, which then stood at around 18,500 units:

Crew wages	£51,766,084
Fuel	£48,001,655
Water	£2,025,314
Clothing	£1,560,060
Miscellaneous	£1,419,587
Lubricants	£543,499
Total	£105,316,199

At a time of cheap oil, full employment, and increasing concern as to atmospheric pollution, the steam locomotive quite simply priced itself out of business.

Bibliography

A. BR Standard Locomotives.

British Railways Standard Steam Locomotives by E.S. Cox, Ian Allan Limited, 1966.
A Pictorial Record of British Railways Standard Steam Locomotives by E. Talbot, Oxford Publishing Company, 1982.
The Riddles Standard Types in Traffic by G. Freeman Allen, George Allen & Unwin, 1982.
Britannia — Birth of a Locomotive by Philip Atkins, Irwell Press, 1991.

B. BR Class 9F 2-10-0s

Ninety With a 'Nine' by W.A. Tuplin, *The Railway Magazine,* December 1958.
The British Railways Class 9 2-10-0s by P. Ransome-Wallis, *Trains Illustrated,* September 1959 and November 1959.
Heavy freight-or express passenger; the BR Class 9 2-10-0 by '45671' in *Trains Illustrated Annual 1960,* Ian Allan Ltd.
The British Railways Class 9 2-10-0 in *Locospotter's Annual 1960,* Ian Allan Ltd.
The BR 2-10-0 Locomotive by Brian Reed *Great Trains Part I,* New English Library c.1972.
Loco Profile 33, BR Class 9F 2-10-0 by Brian Reed, Profile Publications Ltd. 1973.

BR Standard Class 9F, a study of British Railways Standard Class 9F 2-10-0 heavy freight locomotive, ed. G. Weekes, D. Bradford Barton Ltd. 1975.
Locomotives Illustrated, Their Life & Times No.5, 9F 2-10-0s, Ian Allan Ltd. 1976.
What Happened to Steam, Vol 12, The BR Standard 9F 2-10-0s by P.B. Hands, published by the author 1980.
Riddles and the 9Fs by H.C.B. Rogers, Ian Allan Ltd. 1982.
Locomotives Illustrated 75, BR 9F 2-10-0s, Ian Allan Ltd. 1991.

Periodicals consulted: *The Locomotive, Railway Carriage & Wagon Review, Modern Railways, Railway Observer, Railway Magazine, Railway World, Trains Illustrated.*

Other sources (held in National Railway Museum Library): BR Engine History, Boiler & Tender Record Cards, Test Reports. Rugby Locomotive Testing Station files and reports. Minutes of the (BR) Standard Locomotive Committee.

Authors Note:
The photographs ascribed to the R.Partridge Collection were originally made from British Railways official negatives (Derby sequence) which have only recently been transferred to the care of the National railway Museum, but have not yet (1993) been transported to York. For this reason these photographs are not currently available from the museum.

No.92220 EVENING STAR in tandem with BR Class 8 4–6–2 No.71000 DUKE OF GLOUCESTER, on display at Marylebone Goods Yard in May 1961, an exhibition to celebrate the Golden Jubilee of the Institution of Locomotive Engineers.